# A DICTIONARY OF CELTIC SAINTS

# A DICTIONARY OF CELTIC SAINTS

## ELIZABETH REES

First published 2012
Reprinted 2019

The History Press
The Mill, Brimscombe Port
Stroud, Gloucestershire, GL5 2QG
www.thehistorypress.co.uk

© Elizabeth Rees, 2012

The right of Elizabeth Rees to be identified as the Author
of this work has been asserted in accordance with the
Copyrights, Designs and Patents Act 1988.

All rights reserved. No part of this book may be reprinted
or reproduced or utilised in any form or by any electronic,
mechanical or other means, now known or hereafter invented,
including photocopying and recording, or in any information
storage or retrieval system, without the permission in writing
from the Publishers.

British Library Cataloguing in Publication Data.
A catalogue record for this book is available from the British Library.

ISBN 978 0 7524 6305 6

Typesetting and origination by The History Press
Printed and bound by TJ International Limited, Padstow, Cornwall

# CONTENTS

*Preface* 6
*Introduction* 7

The Saints 13
Maps 149

*Further Reading* 153
*Index of Place Names* 155

# PREFACE

This is, so far as I know, the first dictionary of over 100 British Celtic saints, illustrated with photographs of places where each one lived and worked. These range from ruined monasteries to holy wells, from caves to Roman and Celtic forts. This is by no means a comprehensive guidebook: there are very many saints whose cult was quite local, since any Christian who was good and had also died might be considered a saint, and so most monks and nuns qualified for this distinction. This book is therefore a taster and, hopefully, an encouragement to explore further. At the end of the book, some maps and an index enable the reader to explore their local area, or wherever they may find themselves on holiday, in order to track down the saints who were there before them.

We know relatively little about the Celtic saints, since their lives were mostly written centuries later and are therefore to be treated with caution. I have attempted to indicate where legend takes over from fact, but this is rather a grey area. I thank Dr Jonathan Wooding of the Centre for the Study of Religion in Celtic Societies at the University of Wales, Lampeter, for his help and advice over the years. Any errors are my own. My final word of thanks is to the Celtic saints who have enticed me to meet them 'at home' in the beautiful locations where they chose to live around the shores of Britain.

*Elizabeth Rees*

# INTRODUCTION

In order to look at the Celtic saints, we must first ask: who were the Celts? The ancient civilisation of the Celts flourished for over a thousand years. In the fifth century BC, Greek writers described Celts living in the upper Danube region. The Celts conquered Rome in 386 BC and Delphi in 279 BC. When St Paul wrote to the Galatians in western Turkey, they spoke a Celtic language. The Celts were found in Gaul and Spain, and they moved westwards from France and the Low Countries into Britain, as the Germanic tribes and the Romans expanded their territories on the European mainland.

Celtic society was tribal, with elected chiefs who presided over tribal assemblies. Chiefs were also judges and commanded the army in time of war. Druids were professional teachers and priests, trained in tribal law and administration; monks later took over much of their work. Bards were storytellers, poets and minstrels. Druids and bards appear to have become Christian priests and monks. The Celts easily absorbed Christianity: they already believed in immortality and in the sacredness of creation. It has become a cliché to say that the Celts worshipped a triune god, but we still acknowledge this fact, although the Christian concept of the Trinity consisting of Father, Son and Spirit was new to these people.

How did Christianity reach the Celts of Western Europe and the British Isles? Christianity entered Britain through traders and travellers, through the Roman occupation and through Christians emigrating from Gaul. There were periodic persecutions: we hear of Alban being martyred in the third century, and of two Christian soldiers named Julius and Aaron executed at Caerleon in south-east Wales. St Alban was venerated throughout medieval times. In St Albans cathedral one can see the watching chamber that monks built in about 1400 in order to pray to their patron saint and also, perhaps, to keep an eye on pilgrims making their offerings at Alban's shrine, built 100 years earlier (see *colour plate 1*).

In 313 the converted emperor Constantine gave Christians freedom to worship. A scattering of church foundations, lead cisterns for baptism and collections of Communion vessels found across Britain suggest that Christianity spread easily in later Roman times. By then there were bishops in the provincial capitals of York, London, Cirencester and Lincoln; they are recorded attending Church Councils in Gaul, Italy and Bulgaria. Small churches have been excavated that were built for soldiers in forts along Hadrian's Wall, and a possible fourth-century church was found in the Roman town of Silchester, 5 miles south of Reading (see *colour plate 2*).

In the English countryside, a number of villas became house churches, as we can tell from their wall paintings and mosaics, which depict Christian themes. Nine miles south-east of Cheltenham in Gloucestershire, Chedworth Roman villa is situated at the head of the sheltered valley of the River Coln. It was occupied in the fourth century and its owners became Christian at some point. The villa's source of water is a spring which flows through a *nymphaeum*, or shrine to the local water spirit, where it is contained in an octagonal pool surrounded by paving slabs (see *colour plate 3*). An apsed shrine containing a small pagan altar was built over it. Three of the slabs which surrounded the pool have the *chi-rho* (the first letters of the name Christ in Greek) and other Christian symbols carved on them, so by then the pool was probably used to immerse candidates for baptism. Christianity may have been a passing phase, however, for later owners turned the slabs over and used them for other purposes.

Baptism might also take place in the villa's living rooms. Excavations at the Roman villa of Bradford-on-Avon in Wiltshire in 2003 revealed that a fifth-century Romano-British landowner converted the chief reception room of his stately home into an apsed chapel with a baptismal font. He might have been the local priest, or indeed Bradford's bishop, since baptism was conducted by bishops at this time. This was a lavishly designed double villa dating from the mid third century, but, after the withdrawal of the Romans from Britain and the subsequent economic decline, money was becoming scarce and the villa's owner built a rather simple baptistery on top of the fine mosaic floor of the reception room. It consisted of a stone font surrounded by a low circular dry-stone wall (see *colour plate 4*), which stood a metre high; it was built while the villa was still roofed. The baptistery's crude, unplastered finish contrasts poorly with the elaborate mosaic on which it stands. Within the circular enclosure a font made of stone, lead or even wood was probably set into the floor. A shallow pit acted as a soak-away or drain. The font would be large enough to allow the candidate to stand knee-deep in water, while the bishop poured water over his head. This post-Roman baptistery within a villa is unique in Britain, but there are parallels in fifth-century Gaul and Italy: there is a similar baptistery at Rennes in eastern Brittany.

In contrast to the humble baptistery, the fine earlier mosaic on which it stands is reminiscent of those found in Tunisia, North Africa. Its imagery recalls Christian themes, which suggests that the space may have initially been designed as a Christian chapel. The baptistery remained in use from about AD 450 until perhaps as late as 650, when St Aldhelm (d. 709) is thought to have established the small church that can be seen today, on a separate site above the river. The villa is set in Church Field, a name which may recall its earlier use; it is now a playing field in the grounds of St Laurence School.

When the Romans withdrew in the first decade of the fifth century, life continued in Britain's rural communities, and a villa was sometimes the nucleus of a later village, as the name implies. Romano-British Christian families appear to have kept their faith alive. The autobiographical *Confession* of St Patrick describes a family from north or west Britain in late Roman times. Patrick tells us that his father was a deacon and his grandfather was a priest.

Many of the early British Christians whom we call the Celtic saints were monks and nuns. This form of life originated in the eastern churches of Syria, Palestine and Egypt, where men and women began to move out of the cities into the desert in order to search for God in solitude. Pilgrims from Europe returned home with stories of how they lived, and soon western men and women began to try out the monastic life for themselves. In the fourth century, Bishop Athanasius of Alexandria wrote a *Life* of the Egyptian hermit, Antony. This was widely circulated, and Antony's pattern of life became a model for early monks and nuns. A medieval statue which may depict Antony of Egypt can be seen to the right of the altar in the late medieval church at Padstow on the north Cornish coast. He is bearded and holds a staff and a hand bell, with which to summon people to pray (see *colour plate 5*). The statue was probably preserved from an earlier church on the site; if it does not depict Antony, it represents the Celtic monk Petroc, to whom the church was dedicated.

The word 'monk' comes from the Greek term *monachos* which means 'one who is alone'. Monks lived in caves or huts, often grouped around a more experienced leader. Bishop Martin of Tours (*c.* 316–97) was the best known of the early western figures who pursued the monastic life. His friend and biographer, Sulpicius Severus, portrayed him as a western Antony. Martin preached widely throughout the surrounding countryside, and is likely to have provided an important model for others in the western Church. Sulpicius Severus describes how the bishop lived in a wooden cell, surrounded by about 80 disciples, who dug out caves or lived in wooden huts, and shared all their possessions. The monasteries of Gaul developed a strong intellectual tradition, and from AD 400 their influence spread to Ireland and Wales.

The Christian tradition of living in caves dates back to the time of the Desert Mothers and Fathers of the Near East. They took literally the words of the Letter to the Hebrews in the New Testament, which describes God's holy ones living in the same manner: 'They were too good for the world and they went out to live in deserts and mountains, and in caves and ravines' (Hebrews 11.38). Around the British coast and its islands there are caves which were used by Celtic saints. In particular, the soft sandstone around the Fife coast created caves in a number of locations, which early Christians used as chapels and as living quarters.

The Gaelic word for cave is *uaimh* (pronounced 'weem'); place names containing this element normally refer to caves in which early Christian hermits lived. The caves of East Wemyss are on the north shore of the Firth of Forth, 5 miles north-east of Kirkcaldy; these red sandstone caves have been inhabited for 6000 years (see *colour plate 6*). There were nine caves here, of which five survive. Three of them contain the largest collection of Bronze Age, Iron Age and early Christian rock carvings in Britain. Unfortunately, vandalism, coal-mining and erosion of the soft sandstone have blocked access to many of the carvings and destroyed others. St Fillan's cave at Pittenweem in Fife (see *colour plate 7*) has two chambers, with a freshwater pool fed by condensation in the left chamber, providing drinking water for its occupant. The altar in the chamber to the right is modern.

The caves of Caiplie are near the small town of Anstruther on the northern shore of the Firth of Forth, 18 miles east of Glenrothes. One can reach the caves by turning off the A917 just west of Anstruther, to the tiny settlement of Barnsmuir, beside the shore. Half an hour's walk along the shore to the south-east, in the direction of Anstruther, leads to Caiplie. The two caves look across the open sea, and were used by monks and hermits from early Christian times until the sixteenth century (see *colour plates 8 & 9*). The monks enlarged the caves, and on the walls of the larger one, named 'Chapel Cave', they carved small crosses some time between 800 and 1000.

In Celtic kingdoms, pastoral care was tribal: parishes had not yet evolved. Many Celtic saints were high-born members of their tribe. They might be sent to a nearby monastery for a good education; later they commanded their people's respect as they spoke about their faith. At the monastery of St Maolcethair (see *colour plate 10*) at Kilmalkedar on the Dingle peninsula in south-west Ireland, a stone on which the alphabet is inscribed was probably intended to teach literacy to students. Priests and bishops were married. They often lived in monasteries, alongside monks and nuns who chose to remain celibate in order to remain free to pray and preach. Craftsmen and their families also lived around a monastic compound, as can be seen in a model of Bede's eighth-century monastery at Jarrow, built above the River Don, 5 miles east of Newcastle-upon-Tyne and only 2 miles from the sea (see *colour plate 11*).

The soil might be turned with a foot plough – these were used in the Scottish Highlands until the 1940s. In Celtic times, their wooden sides were roughened by the addition of large pebbles. A replica of a Celtic pebble-board plough can be seen at Whithorn Heritage Centre, Galloway, in south-west Scotland (see *colour plate 12*). Abbot Adomnán's *Life of Columba* describes the white horse which pulled a cart containing the leather milk churns to the monastic compound; the horse is likely to have resembled the stocky white ponies one can see on Iona today (see *colour plate 13*). Fish traps set around the island's shores may not have been so very different from the creels still found on Traighmòr ('The Great Strand'), east of the Plain of the Monks, in south-east Iona (see *colour plate 14*).

Many Celtic monks, particularly in Ireland, became 'pilgrims for Christ', and left home in search of a solitary place that God would show them, somewhere unknown, where they could be alone with God. Many set sail in light, hide-covered boats, drifting with the wind and currents until they reached their new location. These men and women were not primarily missionaries, but when they settled in a new place, they had a profound impact on local people. Monks and nuns spread and flourished in the Celtic kingdoms of Ireland, Scotland and Northumbria, Wales, Cornwall, and Brittany.

While some monks established communities, others remained as hermits. A typical hermitage can be seen at St Govan's Head on the Pembrokeshire coast; St Govan's tiny oratory is wedged in a narrow cleft halfway down the cliff, and is reached by 52 steps (see *colour plate 15*). It may date from the eleventh century, but its foundations are probably much earlier. The building consists of a simple nave with a stone altar, benches, a *piscina* to contain water, a shelf and a well in the floor, adjoining the north wall, whose water is said to cure eye diseases, skin complaints and rheumatism. The chapel's arched roof with its stone vault is typical of early medieval churches in Pembrokeshire, and probably dates from the thirteenth century. There is a second well, now dry, in a stone well house on the shore below the chapel. According to legend, Govan may have been Gobham, an early Irish monk, who is said to have hidden here from pirates based on Lundy Island, and was buried near the chapel. The site is on a cliff a mile south of Bosherston and 7 miles south of Pembroke, on the south Welsh coast. (To find the chapel, drive past St Govan's Inn, Bosherston. Continue along the Range Road to St Govan's. It is closed when there is firing on the range. Park at the top of the cliffs. The chapel is soon visible down the cliff path.)

Other hermits chose inland sites, such as Roche Rocks in mid Cornwall, 5 miles north of St Austell; *roche* is French for 'rock'. These are a group of granite tors rising to a height of 30m, south of the village. On top of the largest, reached by iron ladders, is a chapel of St Michael, with a priest's room below, licensed in 1409 (see *colour plate 16*). Hermits lived here in medieval times, and there is a local tradition of a leper living in a cell on the Rock. Similarly, there was a tradition of two hermits living on Glastonbury Tor in Somerset (see *colour plate 17*), where excavation revealed hermits' cells from both Celtic and Saxon times; the early hermits may have been associated with a monastery at nearby Street, across the River Brue. In the foreground of the photo is the so-called holy thorn on Wearyall Hill; it was axed by vandals in 2011.

Celtic monks were often high-born; they might be the second son of the local chieftain. His first son would rule after him and his second son might become a holy man, who could read and write and pray. Chieftains sometimes gave a missionary monk part of their fort as a safe place to stay; since Celtic society was tribal, a chieftain's co-operation was essential. A chieftain often had more than one fort, since no region could sustain his hungry warriors for long. Many forts were quite impregnable, such as Tintagel, on a headland high above the Cornish cliffs (see *colour plate 18*).

At first, monks preached at pagan holy places. St Patrick's Chair, in a field in the parish of Marown, near the centre of the southern half of the Isle of Man, is thought to be an early Christian preaching station – a site where the gospel was proclaimed before churches were established (see *colour plate 19*). Its three slabs are set in a cairn of stones, which may originally have formed a pre-Christian dolmen. At some time between 400 and 700, simple crosses were carved on two of the slabs. The site acquired its name much later, since dedications to saints on the Isle of Man are Norse or medieval.

Early churches were built of unmortared stone. The small church named Gallarus Oratory on the Dingle peninsula, overlooking Smerwick Harbour in Kerry, Ireland, is a fine example of this (see *colour plates 20 & 21*). It is the only complete early medieval chapel on the Irish mainland and its shape has been compared with that of an upturned boat. A banked wall demarcates the monastery in which it stood and an inner wall separates the remains of the monks' huts from the oratory. The building perhaps dates from the eighth century and is made from local gritstone. The little church is constructed with unmortared stones, each layer set further inwards to form a curved roof. Its nine ridge stones are still intact. Often a corbelled roof of this design collapses in the middle, its weakest point, unless its masons are exceptionally skilled. Such chapels are almost all found in Kerry. The oratory has a low doorway at its western end, with two large lintel stones and a wooden or leather door hung from the pair of projecting stones inside the chapel. At its eastern end, a small circular window splays inwards to shed morning light on the missal for the priest to celebrate the Eucharist.

In wealthy monasteries, beautiful vessels were created to use when celebrating the Eucharist; therefore metal workers were held in high regard. At Clonmacnoise, an altar is spread with replicas of the few elaborate vessels which have survived from early times, including two chalices, a wine strainer and a pattern, or dish, for the bread. Behind an illuminated missal is a small house-shaped shrine containing relics, or bones of a saint; to the left is a bronze bell (see *colour plate 22*). Sadly, most of these beautiful objects were destroyed by fire, floods, battles, Vikings or during the Reformation. Celtic Christianity and culture was extinguished in lowland Britain by the Saxons and the Normans, but in some of the more remote regions, such as the Scottish Highlands, Celtic monks survived throughout medieval times until the Reformation.

Some of the saints described in this book may not have existed; the name of St Bega, for example, may simply derive from a bracelet (or *beag*), which was revered for its healing properties at St Bees in Cumbria. Several churches are dedicated to Bega, including that of Bassenthwaite, beautifully situated at the foot of Mount Skiddaw, beside Bassenthwaite Lake (see *colour plate 23*). Other popular saints were honoured in medieval times far from the locations where they are known to have worked. For example, Patterdale, at the southern end of Ullswater in Cumbria, means 'Patrick's Dale'. According to medieval legend, Patrick was shipwrecked on Duddon Sands, north of Barrow-in-Furness, and made his way to Ullswater, where he baptised at St Patrick's well (see *colour plate 24*). It is easy to imagine how such local stories arose. The well is beside the A592 near the boat landings at Glenridding; the heavily restored medieval church is a mile to the south. Most, though not all, dedications to Patrick and Brigit on the British mainland are likely to date from late medieval times.

In the nineteenth century, Alexander Carmichael collected poems and prayers sung by farming and fishing communities in the Scottish Highlands and islands which preserve elements of Celtic theology and thought. Beautiful prayers to accompany such everyday activities as lighting the peat fire and herding the cattle are found in Carmichael's *Carmina Gaedelica*.

# THE SAINTS

## Adomnán

The ninth abbot of Iona, Adomnán (624–704) was born in his father's homeland of Donegal, and came from the royal family of the northern Uí Néill. He first trained as a monk under Columba's nephew, Ernán, and became abbot of Iona in 679 at the age of 55. In his early years as abbot, a bishop from Gaul named Arculf visited Iona when he was shipwrecked off the British coast on his way home from a pilgrimage to Jerusalem. Adomnán welcomed him and wrote a book about the holy places, using information from Arculf and other sources. Adomnán presented a copy of his book to the King of Northumbria; Bede drew upon this guidebook, which became widely used throughout Europe.

In 688 Adomnán went to the monastery of Jarrow in Northumbria, where he spent at least a year, and would have met Bede. In the four years after his return to Iona from Northumbria, Adomnán worked on his *Life of Columba*. In 692 he went back to Ireland, where he challenged his former friend, King Finnachta, over an annual payment of cattle tribute. Adomnán cursed King Finnachta, who died three years later. As the ruler of Columba's monasteries in northern Ireland, Adomnán returned in 697 to take part in the synod of Birr. He proposed a law to exempt women, children and clergy from taking part in warfare; his new law also applied in Scotland. Penalties for transgressing it were to be paid to the Columban monasteries.

Adomnán was responsible for the oversight of all the Columban foundations and travelled extensively. On the Scottish west coast, he is honoured on North Uist in the Outer Hebrides, and a chapel was dedicated to him on the Isle of Bute, at Kildavanan. Adomnán spent time among the Picts, east of the Grampian Mountains; he maintained a good relationship with the Pictish royal house and is commemorated throughout Pictish lands, especially in Aberdeenshire, Banff and Forfar.

In his old age, Adomnán is said to have worked among the Picts in Glen Lyon, one of the Highland routes leading eastwards towards Loch Tay. Beside the River Lyon, near the Bridge of Balgie, is Milton Eonan ('Mill town of Adomnán'). The nineteenth-century church at Innerwick, on the other side of the bridge, contains a Celtic hand bell, known as the Benrudh Bell; it is said to have belonged to Adomnán. It was lost for 200 years in the churchyard and then recovered. Eight miles to the east,

*Wheel-headed cross, Old Kirk Lonan, Isle of Man.*

where the valley broadens, the church of Dull is dedicated to him. There was a famous monastery here, possibly founded from Iona; it remained a centre of learning for many centuries. Closer to Innerwick is a small hill named Camusvrachan, traditionally the place where, when plague struck, Adomnán prayed with the people and sent them up to their summer shielings, away from the polluted river; the plague then ceased. Adomnán returned to Iona, and died shortly after his final visit to Ireland.

In Ireland and Scotland, Adomnán's name was shortened to 'Onan', and Old Kirk Lonan in Onchan parish on the Isle of Man is a medieval dedication to Adomnán. In the churchyard an impressive wheel-headed cross stands in its socket stone, probably in its original position; it is decorated entirely with interlacing, knots and plaitwork. It stands 1.5m high and measures 1m across; it dates from the ninth or tenth century.

# Aidan

Aidan of Lindisfarne (d. 651) was largely responsible for introducing Christianity to Northumbria; our chief source of information about him is Bede's *Ecclesiastical History of the English People*. Writing in about 731, Bede was able to draw on the knowledge of elderly monks in his community when he describes Aidan's work. Bede tells us how he arrived from Iona at the king's request to convert his subjects:

> When King Oswald asked for a Scottish bishop to preach the gospel to himself and his people, first another man was sent, an austere man who was unsuccessful. The English people ignored him, so he returned home, and reported to the assembled council that he had been unable to do any good among the people to whom he was sent to preach. They were uncivilised, stubborn and barbarous. (Bede, bk 3, ch. 5)

The monks gathered on Iona, discussed what to do, and an Irishman named Aidan suggested that the previous missionary bishop might have been too severe. The community therefore decided to consecrate Aidan as bishop and sent him to Northumbria instead.

Aidan arrived with 12 companions in 635. Bede describes Aidan with affection and admiration. He did not approve of the Irish bishop's method of calculating Easter, but he praised his love of prayer and study, his gentleness and humility, and his care for the sick and the poor. Bede's unusually lavish words may have been intended as a reproof for the lax bishops of his own time. He relates:

> When [Aidan] arrived, at his request the king gave him the island of Lindisfarne for his bishop's seat. Here the tide ebbs and flows twice a day, so the place is surrounded by the sea and becomes an island. Again twice a day, the shore becomes dry and is joined to the land … The bishop was not skilled at speaking English, and when he preached the gospel, it was most delightful to see the king himself interpreting God's word to his commanders and ministers, for he had learnt to speak fluent Gaelic during his lengthy exile. (Bede, bk 3, ch. 3)

Oswald had spent his youth on Iona, when his uncle seized the throne in 616. King Oswald lived in a fortress on a rocky outcrop at Bamburgh, 15 miles south-east of the present town of Berwick-upon-Tweed. From Bamburgh, Aidan's island monastery of Lindisfarne was just visible, 6 miles up the coast. Oswald ruled for only eight years; at the age of 38 he was killed in battle by the pagan King Penda of Mercia.

Bede tells us how Bishop Aidan lived: he preferred to travel on foot rather than on horseback, and engaged people in conversation. If they were pagan, he taught them about Christianity; if they were believers, he encouraged them. Aidan spent each Lent on the Farne Islands, about 2 miles offshore, for 40 days of solitude. He was on Farne when King Penda ravaged Northumbria and reached the royal stronghold at Bamburgh. His soldiers set fire to the fortress, and Aidan, seeing the flames from his cell on Farne, prayed until the wind changed direction and the flames engulfed Penda's troops, who were forced to retreat. Among Aidan's friends and followers were a number of

*Lindisfarne priory ruins.*

women, including Oswald's half-sister, Princess Ebbe, who became a nun at the double monastery for both men and women at Coldingham. Another of Aidan's friends was Hilda, who became abbess at Whitby, where her double monastery became a centre of learning and the arts. Aidan became ill and died in his church at Bamburgh. He had been bishop of Northumbria for 16 years.

Little survives on Lindisfarne from Aidan's day: the monastery was destroyed by Vikings in 793 and the monks left the island a generation later, dismantling their wooden church and taking its timbers with them. The surviving priory ruins date from the twelfth century. The nearby parish church of St Mary may stand on the site of a second Anglo-Saxon one. South-west of the priory is a rocky islet which Cuthbert used as a retreat. At low tide it is 10 minutes' walk from the priory, but at high tide it is cut off from the mainland. There are remains of a medieval chapel on the island; its ruined walls are covered with pink thrift and yellow birdsfoot trefoil in summer. At its east end, a tall wooden cross marks the site of the altar. More fragmentary stones may be the remains of Cuthbert's hermitage.

## Asaph

Asaph was the grandson of Pabo Post Pryden, King of north Britain. He is known largely through a late *Life of Kentigern*, whose disciple he became as a youth. His dedications are chiefly found in Flintshire, where Llanasa may have been his base. When Kentigern left Wales and returned to Strathclyde in the late sixth century, we are told that he placed Asaph in charge of his monastery of Llanelwy, later named St Asaph. At a time when waterways were as important as roads, Llanelwy was in a key position at the junction of the rivers Elwy and Clwyd; it is near the north Welsh coast and 5 miles south of Rhyl, and was therefore also easily accessible from the sea.

According to Kentigern's twelfth-century biographer, Jocelyn of Furness, he 'went through the area, exploring different places, bearing in mind the air quality, the fertility of the soil, the suitability of the fields, pasture and woodland, and the other requirements for a monastic site'. Once the location was chosen, 'some cleared the ground and levelled it, while others dug the foundations. They chopped down trees, transported them and hammered planks together to build a church following Kentigern's plan, and made wooden polished furniture, for the British did not yet build in stone.' In the twelfth century, the Normans made St Asaph the cathedral of a diocese centred upon the kingdom of Powys. The present building dates mainly from the thirteenth century; it is set on the hillside above the river valley.

The church at Llanasa, whose name means 'church site of Asaph', is dedicated to saints Asaph and Cyndeyrn; Cyndeyrn is Welsh for Kentigern. The village is in a sheltered valley near the north Welsh coast, 6 miles east of Rhyl. The present double-chambered church was built in the fifteenth century; an asymmetrical bell turret was constructed at this time. In 1540, when the monasteries were dissolved at the Reformation, two fine stained-glass windows were brought to Llanasa church from Basingwerk abbey in Holywell. The window over the altar depicts four saints, including Beuno dressed as a bishop. The saint to his right is Beuno's niece,

*Bell turret, Llanasa.*

Winifred, with a scar round her throat, although she is named, probably incorrectly, as St Catherine. The church also contains the fourteenth-century tombstone of the father of Owain Glyndwr, the last Welsh fighting prince who rose against the English and died in 1416.

## Bega

Bega was a legendary seventh-century Irish nun; St Bees on the Cumbrian coast is named after her. Her cult may have arisen from the bracelet preserved until the twelfth century at her shrine in St Bees, that was said to have healing properties. Its Old English name, *beag*, may have suggested the saint's name. She may or may not be the nun Begu (d. 660) of Hackness in north Yorkshire who, according to Bede, saw in a vision the death of Hilda, who founded the communities of both Hackness and Whitby. A hymn in a fifteenth-century book of hours in the Bodleian Library, Oxford, describes Bega as an Irish chieftain's daughter who vowed chastity. She escaped before an arranged marriage and fled across the sea, landing at St Bees, where she founded a convent. There is a church dedicated to Bega beside Lake Bassenthwaite, at the foot of Skiddaw (see *colour plate 23*), and a church and holy well are named after her at Kilbucho in the Upper Tweed valley. She is also honoured at Dunbar on the coast, east of Edinburgh. Bega is the subject of the novel *Credo* by Melvyn Bragg, which conveys a lively impression of the society in which the Celtic saints lived and worked.

The Norman priory of St Bees on the Cumbrian coast was founded by monks from the great Benedictine abbey of St Mary's, York. Norsemen arrived here in the eleventh century and called the settlement *Kirkeby Begoc* ('the village near Bega's church'). The fine west door of St Bees priory is decorated with chevrons and beak-heads

*St Bega's cave, Fleswick Bay.*

of grotesque birds or beasts; it was built in about 1160. Inside, the nave pillars date from around 1220. There is an early Christian cross in the graveyard, opposite the great west door, and inside is the stump of a fine carved cross dating from the tenth or eleventh century. An hour's walk westward around the cliffs brings one to Smuggler's Cave in Fleswick Bay. According to legend, this is where Bega took shelter after reaching the Cumbrian coast in her flight from Ireland.

## Beuno

Beuno is one of the few known Celtic monks who lived and worked in north Wales. His *Life* survives only in a fourteenth-century translation of a lost Latin original, but some elements in it appear to be genuine. Beuno was born of a noble family in mid Wales in the second half of the sixth century. He was said to have trained for the priesthood in one of the great monasteries of south Wales, and returned to his father's territory of Powys. According to Beuno's *Life*, after his father's death, a local prince gave Beuno the small settlement of Berriew, 5 miles south-west of present-day Welshpool, as a site for his first monastery. Its name (*Aber Rhiw* in Welsh) indicates that Berriew grew beside the River Rhiw where it flows into the Severn, near the Roman road to Wroxeter. Beuno's church is set in a Celtic oval churchyard; it was rebuilt in the nineteenth century.

There is a monolith known as *Maen Beuno* ('Beuno's Stone'), a pointed Bronze Age standing stone in Dyffryn Lane, a mile from Berriew church. This perhaps marked the settlement's ancient holy place and here, according to tradition, Beuno preached to the people at the beginning of his missionary career. To reach it, drive through Berriew, passing the Red Lion Inn on your right. At the junction with the A483, continue across the main road into Dyffryn Lane (unsigned), past a few houses and a layby. Beuno's Stone is on the right, beside the hedge.

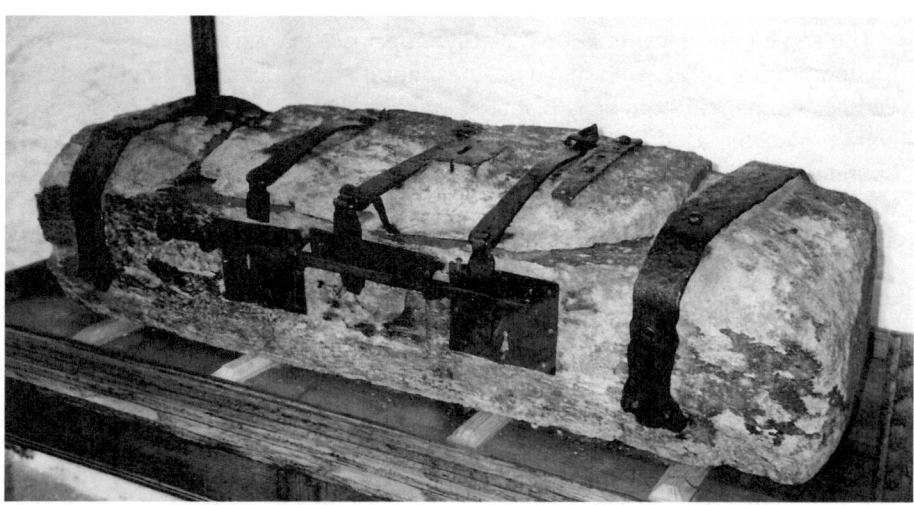

*Beuno's chest, Clynnog Fawr.*

Beuno's *Life* describes how he remained in Berriew for some years until he was frightened by the sight of a Saxon warrior patrolling on the far side of the Severn. In the face of the advancing English, he decided to move to safety, and travelled north-west through the Berwyn Mountains into the valley of the River Dee. Here there is a cluster of dedications to him around the village of Gwyddelwern, where he is said to have founded a community.

There is another group of churches and holy wells named after Beuno near the Flint coast. Beuno was said to be the uncle of Winifred and, according to her *Life*, he obtained land from her parents at Holywell, where he also built a church. His *Life* recounts how he later travelled 50 miles west along the coast to Caernarfon, where he asked the chieftain, Cadwallon, for a site on which to build a church. Cadwallon offered him land that belonged to someone else, after which Beuno cursed him angrily. Cadwallon's cousin, Gwyddaint, then gave him part of his own township of Clynnog, 10 miles further along the coast. Around 616 Beuno established a monastery here, where he spent the last phase of his life. From here, Beuno or his followers travelled along the Lleyn peninsula and visited Anglesey, where a number of churches are named after Beuno and his disciples. He is said to have died in Clynnog at the end of Easter week in 642.

The small free-standing chapel beside the impressive church of Clynnog is probably built on the site of Beuno's church, and may have contained his tomb. Until the eighteenth century, pilgrims came here to Beuno's shrine to pray for healing. Outside the chapel of Beuno's grave, a number of early graves of males were found, perhaps of early monks, and a cist (or slab-lined) grave was found in the corner near the tenth-century sundial, which stands beside the outer wall of the chapel. The sundial is carved on the southern face of a pillar stone, pierced with a hole into which the gnomon was inserted to cast its shadow. This is one of Britain's earliest sundials, and would have been used by the monks in their ordered life of work and prayer. It was returned to the church after being used for other purposes on two different farms.

The settlement became known as Clynnog Fawr ('Great Clynnog'); the name Clynnog means 'place with much holly', although holly does not grow much here. Perhaps it is named from holly planted alongside the monastery's enclosure wall as extra protection, as at Iona. Only the western half of the enclosure survives today, bounded in part by a stream flowing from Beuno's holy well. A large medieval church was built alongside Beuno's chapel. It was extended just before the Reformation to accommodate the crowds of pilgrims who came here to begin walking the Saints' Way, a route which led along the Lleyn peninsula to Bardsey Island at its tip.

Inside Clynnog church is 'Beuno's chest', hollowed out from a single tree trunk. People put offerings into Beuno's chest to atone for crimes; they also offered money from the sale of animals which they considered to belong to Beuno. At birth, some Welsh calves and lambs have a slit in their ears, known as 'Beuno's mark' (*Nôd Beuno*), as do Jersey cattle today. Until the late eighteenth century, farmers brought these animals to the churchwardens on the Sunday after Whitsun; they were sold, and the money was placed in the chest. Beuno's well is 200m south-west of the church, beside the main road. A flight of steps leads up to a pool of clear water in a square, open-roofed, stone well house. It supplied water for the monastery and became a famous healing well.

# Blane

Blane was a British monk from the kingdom of Strathclyde who lived in the late sixth century. He was said to have been brought up on the Isle of Bute, where his uncle, Catán, established a monastery at Kingarth. Catán sent Blane to Ireland to train as a monk; he later succeeded his uncle as abbot of Kingarth and bishop of the surrounding area. A number of early churches in western Scotland are named after Blane; he established his chief monastery at Dunblane.

Situated 5 miles north of Stirling, Dunblane means '*dún*, or fort, of Blane'. This hill fort in the land of the southern Picts was built to defend the main route to the north. In the early seventh century, Blane or his followers built a cluster of beehive huts inside the fortress, to the east of the present cathedral, high above the fast-flowing Allan Water. Blane is said to have returned to his island monastery on Bute to die, but his relics were taken to Dunblane, perhaps to preserve them from Viking raids along the west coast in the ninth and tenth centuries. Blane's hand bell is preserved in the cathedral, together with a large tenth-century Pictish cross slab. The twelfth-century belfry was originally separate from the church, and was built for defence as well as for housing bells. It was erected during the reign of King David I, who endowed the bishopric. By the early thirteenth century, the cathedral had become neglected; it was rebuilt by Clement, a Dominican friar who was elected bishop in 1233. The upper storeys of the building were added around 1500.

*Dunblane cathedral in the snow.*

# Boisil

Boisil, the second abbot of Melrose, trained as a monk in Ireland. Bede tells us how Boisil attracted Cuthbert to Melrose: an elderly monk named Sigfrid, from Bede's own monastery of Jarrow, could remember the day in 651 when a youth named Cuthbert rode up to the enclosure gate at Melrose and leapt down from his horse. He handed its bridle to a servant, together with his spear, in order to enter the church and pray. The prior, Boisil, was standing at the monastery door and noted young Cuthbert with approval. He asked why the youth had come, and the 18-year-old replied that he would prefer life in the monastery to life in the world. Boisil welcomed Cuthbert kindly, told the abbot, and received permission for Cuthbert to have his head shorn and be enrolled among the brothers (Bede, *The Life and Miracles of St Cuthbert*, ch. 6).

The town of Melrose is 30 miles south-east of Edinburgh; the ruins in modern Melrose are of a Cistercian abbey founded in the twelfth century. The earlier foundation of *Mailros* (or Old Melrose) was on a bend of the River Tweed, 2½ miles east of the Cistercian abbey. Like many insular monasteries, it was built within an abandoned hill fort. It was probably founded by Aidan of Lindisfarne with monks from Iona, and its first abbot was Eata, one of Aidan's Anglo-Saxon converts.

Boisil died in 661; his body was taken from Old Melrose and enshrined in the abbey of Jedburgh, 42 miles south-east of Edinburgh. Jedburgh abbey is set on a hilltop above the fast-flowing Jedd Water; an Anglian monastery was established here by Aidan of Lindisfarne. A group of monastic sculptors worked here from the eighth to the tenth centuries; some of their carvings survive, including five free-standing crosses and the end panel of a magnificent house-shaped stone shrine, which is

*Section of Boisil's shrine, Jedburgh abbey.*

likely to have been that of Boisil. The panel depicts a tree of life, with birds and animals among swirling vine tendrils. The ruined Norman abbey dates from the twelfth century; it was established by King David I and given to the Augustinian canons.

# Branwalader: see Breward

# Brendan

One of the most popular Irish monks was Brendan (d. c. 575), whose family name, *moccu Altai*, indicates that he belonged to the *Alltraige*, a tribe who lived in north Kerry. Brendan was said to have been tutored by Bishop Erc of Kerry, and to have been one of the 'twelve apostles' who followed the leadership of Finnian of Clonard. He seems to have been one of the many monks who chose the ocean as a focus for their monastic exile. Writing in the seventh century, Adomnán says that Brendan visited Columba on the island of Hinba, off the Scottish west coast.

Brendan established his principal foundation at Clonfert on the west bank of the River Shannon in about 550. He founded a community at Ardfert in Kerry; an island chapel on Inisglora, off the west coast of County Mayo is also dedicated to him. In medieval times, Brendan was considered a patron of sailors, and churches in a number of coastal settlements in Ireland and Scotland are named after him. Brandon Mountain, 953m high, at the western end of the Dingle peninsula, was the centre of his cult; it became a centre for pilgrimage perhaps as early as the ninth century. At the mountain peak are the remains of cells, a chapel and a holy well. On *Crom Dubh* Sunday each July, reviving an earlier tradition, pilgrims climb the mountain to visit the shrine at its summit.

Brendan owed his popularity largely to a medieval monastic romance, written in about 780, named *The Voyage of St Brendan*. According to the story, when Brendan was abbot of Clonfert, he was visited by a monk named Barrind. This traveller had sailed through thick fog and reached the heavenly Jerusalem, full of precious stones, with all its plants in flower and a river flowing across it from east to west. Barrind describes his experience using words from chapters 21–22 of the book of Revelation at the end of the New Testament. Barrind added that he had returned home after a year.

In chapter 2 of the *Navigatio*, (or 'Voyage'), after hearing Barrind's story, Brendan chooses 14 monks from his own community of Clonfert and tells them that he too wishes to sail to this Promised Land. They eagerly volunteer to accompany him, and Brendan returns to his native Kerry to set out. As a good monk, he avoids visiting his parents, in obedience to Christ's challenge of turning one's back on father and mother for the sake of the gospel. Instead, Brendan and his monks pitch their tent above a narrow creek. At Brandon Creek, Brendan builds a curragh, or wooden-framed boat, covered with ox hides. In the boat, he and his fellow monks put up a mast and a sail, with supplies of food and water for 40 days.

They set sail towards the Promised Land and wander the ocean for seven years. The story is an allegory of monastic life with its annual cycle of labour and worship: they follow a circular route and celebrate the great festivals at the same places each year. A monastic steward appears at intervals with provisions for Brendan's monks. Each day is punctuated by the monastic liturgy; in an island paradise, the birds sing hymns and chant vespers and the other liturgical offices. The unknown author of the *Navigatio* describes an island of sheep and a paradise of birds which may be echoes of the Faroe Islands.

St Brendan's cathedral at Clonfert in Galway is 13 miles south-east of Ballinasloe, 2 miles west of the River Shannon. The name Clonfert means 'water meadow of the grave', and well describes the fertile low-lying site where people brought their dead for burial alongside the monks. Brendan is believed to have founded Clonfert in around 558, about 20 years before his death. He is thought to have been buried here. Clonfert was pillaged by the Danes, who sailed up the River Shannon from Limerick and burned the monastery in 1016, 1164 and again in 1179. The earliest surviving feature of the monastery is a cruciform walk of yew trees perhaps planted in the tenth century.

The present cathedral dates from the end of the twelfth century. It is a simple single-chambered building, with *antae*, or pillars, projecting beyond the walls at each gable. These are a feature of early Irish churches, and were designed to support the roof timbers. The chancel was added in the early thirteenth century, and a beautiful, simple east window was added at this time. A door in the north wall of the chancel leads to a sacristy, in which marks of the wattle roof can be seen in the low plastered ceiling.

Clonfert's magnificent west doorway is perhaps the finest example of twelfth-century Irish Romanesque carving. It was constructed under Bishop Peter O'Moore (1161–71). The door is surmounted by a pediment decorated with carved men's heads, set within a geometric design. Some heads are old and bearded, while others are young and clean-shaven. It recalls the ancient Celtic head cult, in which the entrance to a chieftain's stronghold might be adorned with the potent heads of ancestors or foes. Carved around the doorway are a variety of animals' heads, suggesting Scandinavian influence.

As if to illustrate the story of *The Voyage of St Brendan*, a fifteenth-century mermaid is carved on the chancel arch of the cathedral. She lures unwary monks to destruction as she combs her long, sensuous hair, resting a mirror on her naked body. There was a large monastery at Clonfert throughout medieval times until the Reformation. A state paper from the reign of Elizabeth I records that before Trinity College, Dublin, was founded, it was proposed to establish the university at

Clonfert, since at that time it was known as a seat of learning, and it was in a central location for Irish students. However, the monastery and church were destroyed in 1541 and the monastery was never rebuilt. The church was restored in 1641, but once more fell into ruin. It was eventually repaired in 1900.

Brendan's monastery at Ardfert is in his own tribal territory, 3 miles from the Kerry coast. It is 5 miles north-north-west of Tralee. Ardfert means 'Height of the grave', and much of north Kerry is visible from the low ridge on which the monastery was built. An ogham-inscribed stone and some early graves were discovered in the vicinity of the eleventh-century cathedral. Ogham is an alphabet using incised lines grouped along two adjacent edges of a monument; its straight strokes were easier for masons to carve than the curved letters of the Roman alphabet. The greatest number of ogham-inscribed stones is found in southern Ireland, where it is likely that a number of Irish people were competent Latin speakers. The concept of incised commemorative slabs came from the pagan Roman Empire, and ogham possibly pre-dates the arrival of Christianity in Ireland. The inventors of this cipher were familiar with the sound values of spoken Latin, and the alphabet may have been devised by Latin-speaking Irish intellectuals, perhaps as early as AD 300.

A stone church at Ardfert was destroyed by lightning in 1046; some of its masonry survives in the cathedral's north wall. A round tower was built at this time; it collapsed in 1776 and only its base remains. In the twelfth century, Ardfert was declared a diocese. Some time after 1130, a fine Romanesque cathedral was designed, with an imposing west doorway modelled on Cormac's chapel at Cashel. The rest of the cathedral was later rebuilt. There are two smaller churches within the monastic enclosure; the earliest, named *Teampall na Hoe* (or 'Church of the Virgin'), was constructed in the twelfth century. It has a steeply pitched roof and, unusually, columns with carved capitals decorate its outer corners. A second church, *Teampall na Griffin*, was added beside it in the fifteenth century.

*Mermaid on the chancel arch, Clonfert cathedral.*

# Breward

The name of Breward, or Branwalader, means 'Raven Lord'. He was perhaps a Breton saint; he is named in a tenth-century Breton litany. The Saxon King Athelstan founded Milton abbey in Dorset in about 933 in honour of Our Lady, Samson and Branwalader and gave it the arm of Bishop Branwalader, together with relics of Samson, perhaps obtained from Brittany. Breward's cult was well established in medieval times. He is the patron saint of St Breward in Cornwall, of St Brelade in Jersey and perhaps of St Briavels in Gloucestershire. St Breward is a hill-top settlement, 200m above sea level, situated on the western side of Bodmin Moor, 4 miles south of Camelford, An unusual tenth-century wheel cross, decorated with trefoil shapes carved out between each arm, stands in the lower churchyard. The church contains solid Norman pillars with fluted capitals and a Norman font.

The old church of St Brelade in Jersey is perched above a sheltered harbour; it stands on a rocky shelf overlooking the bay. Descending down to the shore is a flight of sanctuary steps; these are ancient granite steps leading to a slipway on the beach below. Criminals could seek safety in the church and then flee from the island by descending to a waiting boat. The churchyard was formerly roughly circular, with the cliff forming a third of its boundary. Its situation is unique among Jersey churches, but typical of Celtic sites. A Norman parish church stands alongside a smaller chapel, named the Fishermen's chapel. The present chapel dates from the twelfth century, with fourteenth-century wall paintings. In the 1970s Dr Warwick Rodwell excavated and restored the buildings. It became evident that this had been a pre-Christian holy site: there were Neolithic flints on the rock shelf and megaliths that were no longer in situ. A standing stone was found partly under the south transept of the church, where it had apparently been used as the threshold of an earlier timber church. Similar stones were recorded in the foundations of the chancel.

The small areas of topsoil that were excavated contained the remains of timber structures and domestic debris, potentially medieval. Cutting through these was a series of shallow, ledged graves

*Tenth-century wheel cross,*
*St Breward, Cornwall.*

which may have accompanied a timber building with a clay floor that pre-dated the Fishermen's chapel; this is likely to have been the original church. It was superseded in the early Norman period by the new and larger parish church, on flatter ground, further back from the cliff edge.

# Brigit

Many traditions but few certain facts have come down to us about the life of Brigit. She lived two generations after Patrick and died around 525. She is believed to have been born some 30 miles west of Dublin, near Kildare. In about 480 or 490 the King of Leinster gave her land at Kildare (meaning 'church of the oak'), where she built a monastery beneath an ancient holy tree, which survived until the tenth century; the monastery soon grew in importance, and Brigit's early *Lives* were written to enhance its fame. Brigit had a reputation for generosity, and Kildare came to be known as 'the city of the poor'. An early Irish *Life of Brigit* describes her travelling around the countryside in a chariot; its driver was a priest who could baptise the people to whom they preached.

Around 650, a monk named Cogitosus wrote a biography of Brigit that provides us with a valuable description of Kildare 100 years after her death. He speaks of a double community of monks and nuns presided over by an abbess. He tells us of an elaborately decorated wooden church which contained the shrines of Brigit and Conleth, a hermit and metalworker whom Brigit invited to make church vessels for the monastery, and to be pastor for the surrounding people. The two shrines, on either side of the altar, were adorned with precious metals and gems. There were crowns of gold and silver hanging above them, and the church also contained images, paintings and partition walls made of boards.

Brigit's relics were venerated at Kildare until it was raided by the Danes in 836. Little survives of the Celtic monastery except the remains of a high cross and a round tower. Just south of the thirteenth-century cathedral, the foundations of a rectangular building were uncovered in 1966. Now named the Fire Temple, this may have contained the convent's communal hearth; a street beside the cathedral is named Fire Temple Lane. Brigit owes her name to Brígh, a Celtic goddess of fire and light, and inherited some of her attributes. When Gerald of Wales visited Brigit's convent in the twelfth century, he saw a fire which the nuns carefully tended. He wrote: 'The fire is surrounded by a circular withy hedge, which men are not allowed to enter.' The communal hearth was a central feature of ancient rural communities, and was held to be holy. In monasteries, the fire lit on Easter night might be kept alive for the following year.

Kildare cathedral is set on a low ridge where three roads cross, and Brigit's monastic 'city' became a large one. In the seventh century, Cogitosus described it as 'the chief of almost all the Irish churches'. He added that the king's treasury was in Kildare, and the cathedral must have been worth plundering, for it was raided by the Vikings 16 times. Kildare seems to have been singled out for its wealth, for it was pillaged more frequently than other Irish monasteries. This suggests a steady flow of pilgrims, who donated generous gifts to Brigit's shrine. Gerald of Wales gives

*Brigit's holy well at Tully, near Kildare.*

a glowing description of a fine illuminated manuscript which he called the *Book of Kildare*; it no longer survives, but was in the tradition of the *Book of Kells*.

One of the ancient roads leading to Kildare passes through Tully, a mile south of the city. Here is Brigit's well; its water flows into a stream, the site of the convent's water mill. There is no stream in Kildare, and running water was necessary to turn a mill wheel in order to grind the community's flour. The well is still a place of pilgrimage; it can be found by following a signed road opposite the Irish National Stud. Brigit's well is at the far end of a small meadow; its water flows through a pool, where a stone trough and seats on either side allow pilgrims to bathe. Beside the well, a larch tree is hung with clouties, symbolic prayers for healing. A closer look at the cloutie tree indicates the kinds of cures for which Brigit is invoked: bandages, handkerchiefs, socks, stockings and children's toys form silent prayers for healing broken limbs, crippled feet and sick children. Brigit became a patroness of healers, midwives and new-born babies.

Of the many legends about Brigit, one describes how she was called to the bedside of a dying pagan chieftain. As she sat beside him, she picked up some rushes from the floor, weaving them into a cross, and explained the story of the crucifixion to him. Brigit's crosses are still made, although the tradition probably pre-dates Brigit, since their most ancient form has three arms, not four. In the National Museum, Dublin, there is a shrine made of silver and brass, set with jewels, containing a relic of Brigit's shoe. 'St Brigit's mantle' is found in Belgium, in Bruges cathedral; it is said to have been taken there by the Saxon King Harold of England's sister after the Norman invasion of 1066. It is a small square of red woollen cloth with curly tufts. Such shag-rug mantles were woven in Ireland from Bronze Age times until the sixteenth century.

Brigit was invoked for healing and fertility; she protected cattle and blessed their milk. She inherited these powers from the goddess Brígh, whose festival was celebrated on 1 February, at the beginning of springtime; this became Brigit's feast day. Since Brigit was a popular saint in medieval times she has many dedications across the Celtic world, including various Scottish Kilbrides and numerous Welsh

Llansanffraids ('church of St Bride'). There are a few foundations connected with her early followers, such as Abernethy in Perthshire, and some early dedications at places where Brígh may once have been revered, such as Chelvey, Brean Down and Brent Knoll, three sites on or near the Somerset coast.

# Brychan

In Celtic times, Irish families immigrated to south Wales in search of land. In the fifth century, the family of Brychan landed in south-west Wales and travelled east along ancient routes to the hilly region of Brecon, where they settled. The name Brecon is derived from Brychan. We hear about his life in a document possibly dating from early times which tells how his mother, Marcella, returned to Ireland during a severe winter in order to marry an Irish prince. The frost killed many of the warriors who accompanied Marcella, but her father had had a fur coat made for her and she arrived safely. She gave birth to a son before returning home and named him Brychan, which means 'Little Badger'.

In time, Brychan became the ruler of Brecon. He was said to have married three times and had many children. Ancient lists record 12 sons and 12 daughters, although different versions include different names. Churches dedicated to Brychan's children are found in Wales, south-east Ireland, Devon, Cornwall and Brittany. Some of these may date from early times, but Brychan was popular in medieval times and many more churches were then named after his family. Traditions about Brychan in south-west England are contained in a *Life of Nectan*, written in the twelfth century at Hartland abbey, close to Barnstaple Bay in north Devon. The *Life* portrays Nectan as Brychan's eldest son, although Welsh traditions are different.

*Nectan's holy well at Stoke, near Hartland, Devon.*

# Brynach

According to his *Life*, Brynach was the chaplain or 'soul-friend' of Brychan, and married one of his daughters. His chief church is at Nevern, 8 miles east of Fishguard, near the north Pembrokeshire coast. Another 12 churches are dedicated to him, situated along the ancient routes from Brecon to Ireland, concentrated at the western end, near the embarkation points for Ireland. His title, *Brynach Widdel*, means 'Brynach the Irishman'. In later life, Brynach is said to have become a hermit in the mountains above Nevern, from where Ireland can be seen on a clear day.

Brynach's church in Nevern is at the foot of an Iron Age hill fort. Built on the slopes of Carn Ingli, the crumbling walls and towers of the stronghold dominate the village; the fort is one of the best preserved in Wales. Its chieftain gave Brynach land for a church, with the Caman brook as a boundary between them. This was an important religious centre in early times, with a collection of carved crosses dating from about 400, at the end of the Roman occupation, onwards. There are two fifth-century gravestones with inscriptions both in Latin and in Irish ogham. Set into a windowsill in the nave, one of the bilingual tombstones bears the following inscription: '[the monument] of Maglocunus, son of Clutorius.' The slab was erected to the memory of the Welsh chieftain, Maelgwyn. Outside the church to the east of the porch, a second bilingual stone commemorates a Christian named Vitalianus. Beyond the south transept stands a great cross, 4m high, carved in the tenth or eleventh century, covered with elaborate knot-work panels; it is one of the finest in Wales.

*Elaborate carved cross, Nevern churchyard.*

# Buite

Buite mac Brunaigh was an Irish monk who founded the monastery of Monasterboice in County Louth, near the east coast of Ireland, in about 500. He was described as a bishop, a follower of St Patrick, who healed many people. The ruined monastery is near the Irish Sea coast on R168, 6 miles north-west of Drogheda; it may have been a pre-Christian site. It is known in Gaelic as *Mainistir Bhuithe*, or 'Buite's monastery', and is the only Irish place name containing the Latin element *monaster*, or monastery. After Buite's death in about 521, this became a centre of learning; one of its most renowned scholars, Flann, died in 1056. The Irish annals list the deaths of 22 of its abbots between 759 and 1122, and mention a probable occupation by Vikings in about 968. They were expelled by Donal, High King of Tara, who, it is recorded, killed at least 300 Vikings in the process. The monastery remained in existence until 1122.

Monasterboice boasts two of the finest high crosses in Ireland, both dating from the ninth century, and a ruined round tower over 30m high without its cap, one of the tallest in Ireland. Round towers were built in the ninth, tenth and eleventh centuries by monks throughout the country as defences against Viking attacks. They had no keystone for enemies to pull out, so they could not be demolished as speedily as conventional buildings. Due to their height, they were excellent lookouts. Since their doorways were several metres from the ground, a ladder could be pulled in when the monks were under attack. The only drawback was that if a burning arrow pierced the floorboards inside, the whole column acted as a chimney and became a blazing inferno. When the round tower at Monasterboice was gutted by fire in 1097, much of the monastery's library and its church treasures were burnt; they had been brought there for safety.

Close to the round tower is the west cross; it is unusually tall at 6.4m high. It is richly decorated with 22 panels depicting scenes from the Old and New Testaments. Near the entrance to the graveyard is the south cross, probably commissioned by Abbot Muiredach, who died at the monastery in

*Muiredach's cross, Monasterboice.*

844; an inscription reads 'A prayer for Muiredach, by whom this cross was made'. Punctuating the inscription are carvings of two cats: that on the left fondly licks her kitten, while that on the right clutches a bird that it has just killed. The principal theme of the cross is Christ, Lord of Heaven and Earth. Unusually, the crucified Christ is depicted naked. Two angels support his head so that it does not hang in symbolic defeat. The four sides of the cross are richly decorated with scriptural themes and abstract patterns.

There is a third ruined cross in the north-east corner of the compound, believed to have been smashed by Cromwell's forces. Beside it is a granite sundial of uncertain date; it enabled the monks to determine times of worship. Within the enclosure there are also two ruined thirteenth-century churches. They probably had no connection with the monastery, which had by then ceased to function.

## Buryana

Buryana's Cornish name, *hi beriona*, means 'the Irish lady', so she may have been an Irish nun. Her church site at St Buryan, 5 miles south-west of Penzance, is an ancient one. Excavation has shown that the circular churchyard lies within a Romano-British earthwork, probably an enclosed farm. The twelfth-century martyrology of Exeter cathedral states that the son of the eighth-century Cornish King Gereint was cured of paralysis at Buryana's intercession. According to traditions collected by John Leland in the sixteenth century, the Saxon King Athelstan of Wessex founded a collegiate church here as the result of a vow. In 930, on his way to the Scillies to conquer its inhabitants, he vowed that if he was successful, he would build a new church in Buryana's honour. The stone arches of a magnificent tenth-century church can be seen in the north wall of the later chancel.

Athelstan may have commissioned the fine cross in St Buryan churchyard. Above a panel of decorated knot-work, Christ reigns from the cross, a triumphant warrior, clothed and booted, with arms outstretched to save. The Saxons held fighting in high regard and, according to their theology, Christ was a

*Runhol's cross, St Buryan churchyard.*

young warrior hero. The sculptor carved two similar crosses, one at nearby Sancreed, 2 miles north of St Buryan, and another now at Lanherne, near St Mawgan-in-Pydar, 5 miles north-east of Newquay. On these, he inscribed his name, Runhol.

Buryana's holy well is in a field a mile north-west of St Buryan, in the hamlet of Alsia. It provided the village with drinking water and was also a healing well. Mothers came from far and near with weak and rickety children to bathe them in the well. A nineteenth-century miller's daughter from Alsia recalled that village women fought with the pilgrims to prevent them from dipping their babies into the well and contaminating the water. The well is on Lower Alsia Farm, whose owner welcomes visitors to the well. As the road runs through the hamlet, a flight of steep stone steps leads up through the hedge. Cross two fields, walking diagonally to the right, and the well is now visible, above a small stream. It is contained in a simple stone well house.

# Cadfan

The twelfth-century *Book of Llandaff* desribes a Breton monk named Cadfan, who sailed to mid Wales in the sixth century with 12 followers and settled beside a spring on the seashore at Tywyn, halfway between Barmouth and Aberystwyth. Here they founded a monastery and were joined by many brothers. Near the shore, towards the northern end of the town, the solid yet spacious church dates from the late eleventh and early twelfth centuries. A chapel dedicated to Cadfan stood at the north-east end of the churchyard until 1620; it may have contained his shrine. Cadfan's holy well is north-west of the church, and

*St Cadfan's church, Tywyn.*

can be found in the grounds of the NatWest bank. The spring was visited for healing until long after the Reformation. Baths and changing rooms were built alongside it; they were pulled down in 1894, by which time they had fallen into disuse.

Inside the church, an eighth-century grave marker commemorates two women from leading families; another may indicate the burial place of Cadfan, since it reads in translation: 'Beneath a similar mound lies Cadfan; sad that it should enclose the praise of the earth. May he rest without blemish.' This is one of the earliest examples of written Welsh; until this point, inscriptions were normally in Latin. The inscribed panels are set low down on the shaft, perhaps to be read while kneeling. Two successive wooden churches were burnt by the Vikings. By the mid tenth century, St Cadfan's had become the mother church of the area. Twenty miles to the east, Cadfan is honoured at Llangadfan, a small church high above the River Banwy. A number of churches in mid Wales are named after his followers. Cadfan is also said to have established a monastery on Bardsey Island, beyond the tip of the Lleyn peninsula.

## Cadoc

Cadoc was a leading figure among the monks of south Wales in the early sixth century. When the Romans withdrew from Britain in the early fifth century, local dynasties of Welsh chieftains ruled. Cadoc sprang from one of these dynasties, and a number of churches named after him are associated with Roman forts and settlements. The two earliest biographies of Cadoc, written 500 years after his death, are unreliable collections of legends. We are told that Cadoc was of noble birth: his father, to whom Newport cathedral is dedicated, was a prince of Gwent in south-east Wales. Cadoc's mother, Gwladys, was said to be a daughter of Brychan, the ruler of Brecon, which lies to the north-east of Gwent. Cadoc worked among the descendants of Romano-British Christians. The twelfth-century *Life of Cadoc* describes him as coming from an imperial Roman family, loving the works of Virgil and regretting that, as a Christian, he would be unable to meet the pagan poet in heaven!

There is a cluster of churches dedicated to Cadoc in the upper Usk valley, centred on Llangattock-nigh-Usk ('church of Cadoc near the Usk') in his father's territory, 5 miles north-west of Abergavenny. As a youth, Cadoc is said to have studied at Caerwent, 9 miles east of Caerleon, in a monastery founded by an Irish monk named Tathan. Caerleon's church is also named after Cadoc; it is at the centre of the old town. Part of a ninth-century high cross survives, decorated with bird-like angels and interlaced patterns. It stood at the crossroads outside the churchyard. The Roman ruins in Caerleon provided immense supplies of good building stone and almost all the town's older buildings utilise recycled Roman material. Incorporated into the fifteenth-century tower of Cadoc's church are red sandstone blocks, orange brick tiles and yellow freestone, all of Roman origin. Cadoc's church at Caerleon is built over the Roman *principia*, or legionary headquarters. Cadoc later established a monastery of his own at Llancarfan, 4 miles north-west of Barry, in the Vale of Glamorgan, and a group of monks from Caerwent was said to have joined him.

*Oak rood screen, Llancarfan.*

There were several great monasteries in the area, including that of Illtud at Llanilltud Fawr, only 5 miles to the west of Llancarfan, and that of Docco at Llandough, now a northern suburb of Penarth, further to the east. Llancarfan was beside a stream, not far from the sea, which has now receded. It may have been an ancient port, safely upstream, hidden from pirates. The Celtic monastery probably lies below the field to the south of the medieval church; a well in the next field was also associated with the monastery.

The medieval *Life of Cadoc* by Lifris of Llancarfan describes how, before selecting his site, Cadoc and his monks spent the night in prayer; in the morning a white boar appeared, to indicate where he should begin building. This is a recurring theme in stories of Celtic saints' foundations: the boar was a sacred animal to pre-Christian Celts, and in the lives of Celtic saints a white boar becomes a messenger from God. The pig foundation tales take place in a timeless world of pseudo-history. In the *Life of Cadoc*, a large white boar leaps out from a thicket, frightened by Cadoc's approach. It shows him where to build a church in honour of the Trinity, with a dormitory and a refectory. However, this is an Anglo-Norman pig, for a dormitory, a refectory and a Trinitarian dedication are features of a Norman monastery rather than a Celtic one.

The name Llancarfan means 'church of the stags', from a legend about Cadoc: when he asked two monks to till the ground near the monastery, they refused, but a pair of stags appeared from the woods and dug the soil with their antlers. According to his twelfth-century *Life*, Cadoc was martyred in the late sixth century. While he was celebrating the Eucharist in his old age, in his monastery at Llancarfan, a Saxon warrior entered the church on horseback and pierced him with a lance. The monastery was ravaged by the Danes in 988. After the Norman conquest of Glamorgan in

1090, the monastery was dissolved and the church was annexed to Gloucester abbey. The present church dates from the thirteenth and fifteenth centuries. It contains a fine rood screen of carved oak, dating from the Perpendicular period. In the last few years, medieval wall paintings have been discovered beneath the white wall plaster.

## Carantoc

Carantoc is said to have lived in a cave above the church named after him at Llangrannog on the Ceredigion coast in south-west Wales. Two medieval *Lives* of St Carantoc survive in a manuscript in the British Library, dating from around AD 1200. The first *Life* relates how he came from Ceredigion and founded one or more churches in Britain. The second *Life* connects the saint with the story of how Cunedda and his sons expelled the Irish from Ceredigion.

Little information survives about Carantoc's cult. The most significant foundation named after him is at Crantock on the north Cornish coast: in *Domesday Book*, Crantock is referred to as *Langorroc*, using a hypocoristic or pet form of Carantoc's name. In the sixteenth century, the antiquarian Nicholas Roscarrock related that seven parishes used to bring relics each year to the seven churchyards of Crantock in procession, and each relic was placed on a stone altar. Little evidence survives relating to the monastery at Crantock. There is a holy well in the village dedicated to Carantoc; its conical capped roof is a later addition.

Another medieval church may have been named after Carantoc at Carhampton in Somerset. Its place name may be formed from the Old English words *carrum* and *tun* ('rock town'), but the sixteenth-century antiquary John Leland thought that the place name derived from the saint. By that time it was known as *Carntoun*, which he explained as 'Carantokes towne'. Leland describes two churches, one being the church of St John the Baptist that survives today, and the other 'a chapel of this sainct [Carantoc] that sumtyme was the paroch chirche'.

The location of Carantoc's church remained unknown until

*St Carantoc's well, Crantock.*

1993, when Charles and Nancy Hollinrake excavated an early medieval building at Eastbury Farm on the eastern edge of the village. The site is typical of a Celtic monastery: in an undefended location, on the edge of the alluvial levels, with easy access to the sea. There are suitable landing bays and beaches within half a mile, yet its position renders it invisible to pirates. Unfortunately, torrential rains hindered the Hollinrakes' exploratory excavations, but nevertheless, significant discoveries were made.

Most of the features investigated dated from the sixth to the tenth centuries: timber buildings, a cemetery, and enclosures bounded by ditches. There were four pieces of sixth-century pottery imported from the Mediterranean, including the handle of an amphora and a piece of seventh-century imported pottery, probably from Gaul. Two fragments of early glass were also found; all of these artefacts suggest a high-status site. Nearby was a later enclosed cemetery, in use from the twelfth to the sixteenth centuries. All this probably lay within a large oval enclosure, about 350m long and up to 250m wide.

The position of the early medieval church was deduced from holes for posts, stakes and perhaps timbers. There were early cobbled floors and possible cobbled tracks. A number of finds dated from the fourth and fifth centuries, suggesting that this was a very early site. Its most unusual feature was a large quantity of iron ore and slag. Iron was smelted here, mainly in the sixth and seventh centuries, but continuing into the tenth century. Some of the iron may have been used for smithing in the monastery, but most of it was worked into billets for export. This is the only early British smelting site in the south-west of England and it could be one of the largest so far discovered in England and Wales.

In Saxon times, the three royal estates of Carhampton, Williton and Cannington encompassed the entire north-west Somerset coast between Minehead and the River Parrett. The *Anglo-Saxon Chronicle* records successful Danish raids on Carhampton in the ninth century; the site would have been easy to capture if Carhampton was an undefended monastery. Despite the raids, it continued to be occupied through the Saxon period into the thirteenth century, unlike many other Celtic sites in western Britain. It is tantalising that so much has been discovered from exploratory trenches that were cut prior to the creation of a village bypass that was never constructed.

## Catán

A sixth-century Irish monk who migrated to the Clyde area, Catán founded a monastery on the Isle of Bute. A number of churches in the Western Isles are named after him, and he is honoured at Ardchattan on the shore of Lake Etive. Catán is said eventually to have returned to Ireland, where he died and was buried. At the mouth of the Clyde estuary, Bute was attractive to Celtic monks: it was low lying and fertile, and at the centre of routes from north-east Ireland and south-west Scotland, with Iona to the north-west. The island is sheltered from the ocean, and since it is 5 miles by 15 miles, it could support a considerable population. It is so close to the mainland that sheep and cattle could safely swim across. In Celtic times, the southern end of Bute was the most populous.

There was a fort there and a monastery of some 50 monks with a surrounding settlement. The community was founded by Catán, after whom Kilchattan Bay, a mile to the north, is named. Sources differ as to whether Catán was Blane's uncle or his tutor; as abbot, Catán could well have been both.

Catán's monastery on Bute, now dedicated to Blane, is in a lovely spot in a sheltered valley near the shore. It is surrounded by its original enclosure wall, within which are the remains of a circular fort, a well and the ruins of monks' huts set against a sheltering cliff. In the cemetery are the footings of a small chapel and a few early crosses. There is a stone bowl, perhaps for washing pilgrims' feet in a traditional ceremony of welcome. We hear of various monk bishops who succeeded Catán and Blane, some of whom met violent deaths at the hands of Norsemen.

The monastery was a centre of culture and craftsmanship. A tiny ninth-century crucible for casting bronze brooches was found here, and there are designs engraved on slate which were preparatory sketches made by craftsmen. Norse Christians were buried here: there is a hogback tombstone in the churchyard. A Viking's gold ring was found and a gold fillet for binding a lady's hair. By medieval times the monks had created an inner cemetery for themselves and an outer one for lay people. There are the remains of the medieval church at the centre of the site. A twelfth-century arch separates the chancel from the nave.

In a beautiful setting on the north shore of Loch Etive, St Catán's priory at Ardchattan priory is 8 miles north-east of Oban. The name Ardchattan means 'Catán's hill'. A large Celtic cross slab survives in the priory ruins. The present monastic buildings were constructed in about 1230 by the Vallisculians, who were an offshoot of the semi-eremitical Carthusian order. They also founded Pluscarden and Beauly, further to the north, in Inverness.

*Stone bowl, perhaps for washing pilgrims' feet, Catán's monastery, Bute.*

# Cedd

The short-lived Anglo-Celtic Church of the East Saxons was established by Cedd (d. 664). Bede, our chief source of information about Cedd, tells us that he came from an Anglian family who took their four sons to Lindisfarne to be educated. They became monks under Aidan, who sent them to Ireland for further training. Two became priests and, at the request of Peada, King of Mercia, the other two, Cedd and Chad, came south to be monk bishops in response to a request from Sigbert, King of the East Saxons, who had recently become Christian. Cedd probably landed at the quay of the old Roman fort of Othona, and travelled through Sigbert's kingdom. He returned north to be consecrated bishop and then came south again, building churches at Bradwell, Tilbury and other sites. He was bishop of the area from 654 to 664. Bede describes him 'ordaining priests and deacons to assist him in the work of faith, and the ministry of baptising … Gathering a flock of servants of Christ, he taught them to observe the discipline of regular life, as far as those rude people were then capable' (Bede, *Ecclesiastical History*, bk 3, ch. 2).

On one of Cedd's visits to Northumbria in 658, the king offered him land for a monastery. Bede tells us that the bishop 'chose himself a place to build a monastery among remote and craggy mountains, which looked more like hiding places for robbers and lairs for wild animals than places fit for people to live in' (Bede, bk 3, ch. 3). The site selected by Cedd was Lastingham, 18 miles west of present-day Scarborough. He prayed and fasted there for the 40 days of Lent, before beginning to build. On another visit to the north, Cedd acted as interpreter at the Council of Whitby. Bede informs us that although Cedd followed Celtic customs rather than those of Rome, 'he was in that council a most careful interpreter for both parties' (Bede, bk 3, ch. 23). After the synod, Cedd introduced Roman customs in his diocese. He died of the plague at Lastingham soon afterwards. When his people at Bradwell in Essex heard of this, 30 of them travelled up the coast to pay their respects. All but one, a boy, died of the plague like Cedd.

The chapel of St Peter-on-the-Wall at Bradwell is an outstanding testimony to Cedd's ministry. In Roman times Bradwell-on-Sea was probably Othona, one of the forts of the Saxon Shore, built by the Romans to defend the coastline against the Saxons. The walls of the first fort were 4m thick; its eastern front was probably a quay. This stretch of coast is intersected by many creeks inviting to invaders, and this is one of the few points along the shoreline where the mainland meets the open sea without intervening marshes. A road led to the sea at this point, which probably attracted Cedd to the site in the seventh century, by which time the Roman fort lay in ruins. Cedd built a church across the chief entrance to the fortress, making use of its stone foundations. The Saxons settled mainly towards the quay to the east, beyond the ruined chapel, which was surrounded by a graveyard. *Domesday Book* (1086) records a fishery and salt pans here.

The chapel is perhaps the oldest church in England of which so much remains. St Peter's is one of six seventh-century churches in the Kent region, all built on Roman sites and constructed largely out of recycled Roman material; each had an apse in the Continental style. On his arrival as bishop, Cedd probably built a small

*Chapel of St Peter-on-the-Wall, Bradwell-on-Sea.*

wooden chapel. He perhaps replaced it with the present church as his acquaintance with the region developed. The church is 15m long and 6.5m wide. Its semi-circular apse no longer survives, but it probably contained a cube-shaped altar and a bench round the wall for clergy, with the bishop's throne in the middle.

It appears that there was a double chancel arch, which suggests the existence of a double monastery at Bradwell, in which case the nave would have been divided by a screen or curtain to separate the men from the women. The monks and nuns would have lived in separate buildings under the same superior, as at Whitby, and would have worshipped together, but in separate parts of the same church. There was a sacristy on the north side in which the clergy could vest; it was entered from the apse. A similar room on the south side was used to contain people's offerings in kind; it was entered from the nave. This asymmetrical though logical arrangement was known in the East and in North Africa, but rarely in the West.

## Ciarán of Clonmacnoise

A man of great promise who died young, Ciarán was described by his medieval biographers as the son of an Ulsterman who had settled in Connacht. They record that, unlike many Irish abbots, Ciarán was not of noble birth. They indicate that he was a holy man by stating that, like Jesus, Ciarán was a carpenter's son and died at the age of 33. He was said to have studied under Finnian of Clonard, with Enda on the Aran Islands, and later still with

Senan on Scattery Island in the mouth of the Shannon. Ciarán founded a community on an island in Lough Ree, and later continued downstream along the Shannon, settling at Clonmacnoise. Annals compiled at Clonmacnoise record that this took place in the 540s. The rich pastureland was given to Ciarán by Diarmaid Mac Cerbhaill of the royal house of Uí Néill. Diarmaid helped to build the first wooden church with his own hands, and soon afterwards became high king. Within a year, Ciarán had died of the yellow plague, which swept through Ireland and decimated many communities.

Clonmacnoise is 5 miles south-west of Athlone in County Offaly, in a bend of the River Shannon. Its name means 'water meadows of the sons of Nós'. Ciarán selected a key point on the broad river, near the Athlone ford and on the sandy esker ridge that forms the great east–west road across central Ireland. Today, passing boats are a reminder that the Shannon, Ireland's longest river, was a major route north and south, so Clonmacnoise was situated at the main crossroads of Ireland. The water meadows flood annually and provide rich pasture which could support a large community.

Little survives from Ciarán's monastery. Pieces of sixth-century pottery have been found, and in 1990 an ogham-inscribed gravestone was discovered, perhaps dating from the fifth or sixth century. It is the first to have been found in this region of Ireland; the slab lay beneath the new graveyard, at the eastern end of the monastic site. Further excavation of this area revealed a road, traces of houses, corn-drying kilns and a slipway for boats. At the opposite end of the site, beyond the round tower, underwater excavation carried out in 1994–98 uncovered the remains of a wooden bridge across the Shannon. Tree-ring dating of its oak timbers suggests that it was built in about 804. The construction of a wooden bridge across such a broad river was a remarkable achievement.

Despite Ciarán's early death, Clonmacnoise grew rapidly in importance. Adomnán wrote in his *Life of Columba* (*c.* 690) that when Alither was abbot of Clonmacnoise, Columba paid him a visit. He relates:

> When they heard of his approach, everyone in the fields near the monastery came from all directions. Together with those inside the monastery, they most eagerly accompanied their abbot, Alither. They passed beyond the enclosure wall of the property, and with one accord they went to meet St Columba, as if he were an angel of the Lord.

Adomnán hints here that Iona was rather more important than Clonmacnoise.

By the seventh century, Clonmacnoise had a large non-monastic population, and had acquired many dependent churches. This led to disputes over property. In about 700, Tiréchan, the biographer of Patrick, complained that the community at Clonmacnoise forcibly held many churches which had been founded by Patrick. In spite of their rapturous welcome of Columba, a further dispute arose between the monks of Clonmacnoise and those of Columba's foundation at Durrow, 35 miles south-east. Monks from the two communities fought each other in 764, and 200 men from Durrow were killed.

There was intensive settlement around the monastery, with circular houses where artisans lived with their families: metalworkers in iron and bronze, gold and silver, and craftsmen skilled in antler-working or comb-making. There were also stone masons who, besides carving crosses, produced some 700 grave markers over a period of 400 years. A piece of scratched bone that was used by an apprentice to practise plait-work patterns still survives. His attempts were rather unskilled!

Since Ciarán was not of noble birth and his family were not native to the area, he left no dynasty from which abbots might be chosen. His family was not represented among later abbots, and the monastery remained independent of other clans. Chroniclers in the community kept records of significant events from at least the eighth century, and it is possible to compile an almost complete list of abbots from Ciarán's time until the twelfth century. The settlement's churches were burnt down more than 30 times during this period, by accident, by Irish kings and by Viking raiders.

There are the remains of seven churches and a large cathedral in the enclosure, with three fine crosses and a round tower. Near the centre of the compound is the smallest of the churches, *Teampall Ciaráin*. According to tradition, Ciarán was buried here, and pilgrims used to take home soil from the grave to heal their sick. A relic known as St Ciarán's Hand was kept here until 1684, when the chapel was still roofed. The early tenth-century building has putlog holes in its walls; these held timbers to which scaffolding was tied during the chapel's construction. Its walls are no longer vertical, since so many burials around the founder's tomb have caused the earth to shift.

The round tower stands near the river bank at the west end of the enclosure. Annalists recorded its completion in 1124. However, storms caused damage in the following decades, and in 1135 the top of the tower was torn off by lightning. Close to the round tower is a replica of one of Ireland's most magnificent crosses, the Cross of the Scriptures. The original can be seen in the museum at the site. Its shaft and head were carved from a single piece of sandstone, and an inscription round its base asks prayers for King Flann and for Abbot Colmán who made it. Colmán was abbot from about 904 to 926, and erected the largest of the churches on the site.

Towards the southern end of the enclosure stands the south cross, carved in the ninth century. A damaged

*Clonmacnoise: round tower and Cross of the Scriptures.*

inscription on its base suggests that it was commissioned by the father of King Flann, who is mentioned on the Cross of the Scriptures. Both are made from sandstone, and were probably quarried in County Clare, transported up the Shannon and carved here in the monastic workshops. Much of the south cross is covered with abstract ornament, in the form of interlacing and fretwork, spirals and bosses. This style of decoration appears to derive from earlier metal-encased examples. The elaborate bosses echo the shapes and patterns found on metalwork and jewellery of the period.

Built into the enclosure wall to the north is *Teampall Finghin* (or 'Finnian's church'), dating from 1160–70. The ruined stone church has a unique round tower that also served as a belfry. With frequent raids and a very large community, the monks may have felt the need for this second tower into which they could hurry for protection. The belfry is set at the junction of the chancel and the nave; its conical cap is well preserved. Towards the centre of the site, the cathedral incorporates work dating from the tenth to the fifteenth century, and has a sixteenth-century sacristy. Medieval figures of Patrick and two other saints are carved above the cathedral's great north door.

One of the main approach roads to the monastery from the east leads past the Nuns' Church. It is 500m east of the main site, and stands within a separate enclosure, surrounded by its cemetery. According to the chronicles, there was a stone church here, which was burnt down in 1082. Its remains are incorporated into an adjoining field wall. The annals relate that the present church was completed in 1127 by Dearbhforgaill, wife of the King of Breifne (now Meath). Its ornate west door was restored in the nineteenth century.

Some of the finest scholars of Ireland and Europe studied at Clonmacnoise, including Alcuin, bishop of Tours. The monastery was in a central position and came to rival Armagh in importance. It became the burial place of the kings of Tara and Connaght. The Clonmacnoise crosier, now in the National Museum, Dublin, is believed to have belonged to Ciarán. The ornate metalwork shrine of the *Stowe Missal* (c. 1030) bears an inscription stating that it was crafted by a monk of Clonmacnoise. Some secular texts written by the monks have also survived, including *The Book of the Dun Cow*, which contains the earliest known version of *The Cattle Raid of Cooley* (or *Táin Bó Cuailnge*), a popular Irish saga.

## Ciarán of Saighir

Ciarán is one of the early monks who worked in south-east Ireland before the arrival of St Patrick. He was born on or near Clear Island, off the south-western tip of County Cork, where he is said to have become a hermit, after being baptised and ordained abroad. He later built a large monastery at Saighir, which is now known as Seirkieran, in County Offaly. Here, the kings of Ossory, his family tribe, were buried. The monastery became the seat of the bishops of Ossory. Ciarán is a much-loved local saint and on his feast day, 5 March, pilgrims flock to Seirkieran. The small settlement is 7 miles north of Roscrea and 40 miles north-east of Limerick. Ciarán's monastery is set in rolling hills, with panoramic views in several directions. His *Life* relates how Ciarán tamed a fierce but frightened wild boar that helped him to collect materials with which to build a church. The author adds: 'This boar was the first disciple, as it were a monk of St Ciarán, in that place.' A wild boar often features in the story of a Celtic monk's chief foundation.

Ciarán's *Life* also relates how he decreed that the fire in his monastery must not go out. When it was allowed to do so, and the monks could no longer cook or warm themselves, Ciarán prayed and the fire lit itself again. The communal hearth was a central feature of ancient rural communities and was held to be holy. In monasteries, the fire lit on Easter night might be kept alive throughout the following year. In a number of saints' *Lives*, fire is rekindled at their prayers, to demonstrate God's power. Christian readers would recall that the great prophet Elijah kindled fire through his prayer, after the prophets of Baal failed to do so (1 Kings 18.20–40).

Ciarán's monastery was plundered many times; it later became an Augustinian priory. The walled monastic compound covers 10 acres. There are a few remains of the Celtic monastery: the stump of a round tower, an early grave slab and the base of a high cross. The water which collects in its socket is believed to cure warts. South of the monastery, beside the R421, a signed track leads to Ciarán's well pool. Nearby is Ciarán's Bush, an aged hawthorn tree to which clouties are tied as prayers for healing.

There was also a monastery dedicated to Ciarán at Kilkieran, 5 miles north of Carrick-on-Suir. Its church was on the site where a large later tomb now stands; it was probably surrounded by monks' wooden huts. There are three high crosses at the site; one is unique in design, with its tall thin shaft and stumpy arms, which may have had wooden extensions. The other two crosses are highly elaborate. The ninth-century west cross is particularly fine. On the east side of its base are eight horsemen; the other three sides are decorated with interlacing and geometric patterns.

*St Ciaran's font, Kilkieran, 'good for headaches'.*

Further down the hill are the remains of what may have been a second early church, close to a pre-Christian standing stone. Nearby is Ciarán's holy well; beside it is a boulder with a cavity containing water and known as St Ciarán's Font; its water is believed to cure headaches. In medieval times, Piran of Cornwall was wrongly identified with Ciarán.

# Clether

Listed as one of the sons of Brychan in the twelfth-century *Life of Nectan* written at Hartland abbey, Clether is also mentioned in Welsh traditions. Brychan had a chaplain or soul friend named Brynach, and a twelfth-century *Life of Brynach* describes a chieftain in Pembrokeshire named Clether, who had 20 sons and offered them to Brynach as servants. We are told that the 'righteous old man' then went to Cornwall, where he served God until his death. St Clether is a village on the north-eastern edge of Bodmin Moor in Cornwall, where pilgrims visited the hermit's remote chapel and well in medieval times, and still do so today.

The settlement is on a valley slope above the River Inney, 8 miles west of Launceston. The Norman church stands beside the road above the village. The oval churchyard is surrounded by an embankment, and dates from early times; in the spring, it is carpeted with wild daffodils. To visit the chapel and holy well, walk through the churchyard and continue for half a mile along a signed track which leads through rough pasture and gorse, with a delightful view of the river below. The chapel is built into the rocky hillside, a little below a solid well house constructed over a spring. Its water flows down into the chapel, past three massive granite slabs which form its altar.

Clether's shrine was much visited by medieval pilgrims. In the fifteenth century, the building was altered: an oblong cavity was made in the east wall beside the altar, so that Clether's relics could be housed for veneration. The floor was lowered so that the water could flow through the chapel, behind the granite altar and out into a second pool. A shelf for pilgrims' offerings was constructed above the pool. Behind

*Granite altar, St Clether's chapel.*

the shelf was a small wooden door, which enabled a priest inside the building to retrieve the offerings. With these ingenious facilities, St Clether is the most complete medieval Cornish well and chapel. It was restored in 1895.

## Colmán of Kilmacduagh

Colmán is a Gaelic word meaning 'Little Dove', and there were some 300 Celtic saints named Colmán. The popularity of this name among Irish monks was a standing joke. In one saint's *Life*, a group of monks were working beside a stream when their leader shouted, 'Colmán, get into the water!' and 12 men jumped in. Colmán of Kilmacduagh (d. c. 632) was born in the mid sixth century. He became a monk on Aran Island, off Ireland's north-west coast, and then returned to the mainland, where he settled in the Burren Hills, County Clare. He lived here with a disciple on an austere diet of vegetables and water. Colmán later founded a monastery at Kilmacduagh and was consecrated as a bishop. Part of his crosier is preserved in the National Museum of Ireland, Dublin.

The extensive monastic complex of Kilmacduagh lies 17 miles south-south-east of Galway and 3 miles west-south-west of Gort, on the R460. Kilmacduagh is one of the finest Irish monastic sites, set in green meadows near the shore of a lough, with the Burren Hills on the horizon. Colmán founded the monastery on land given to him by his kinsman, Guaire the Generous, King of Connacht, who lived in Gort and provided the workmen and materials to build the monastery.

The cathedral is the largest building within the enclosure; it occupies the site of a rectangular seventh-century church. The cathedral's west end, with its lintel doorway, roof corbels and steeply pitched gable, was probably built before the eleventh century. Large blocks of stone from the early church can be seen alongside dressed stones of later times. The cathedral's side chapels date from the fourteenth and fifteenth centuries. Colmán was said to be buried in a shrine outside the cathedral. Nearby, the ruined church of John the Baptist dates from the tenth century. The remains of Our Lady's church stand beside the road that was driven through the site in the

*Round tower, Kilmacduagh.*

eighteenth century. Next to St John's church, the Glebe House was the later bishops' residence. It is strongly fortified, with slit windows for defence. Signs of a crenelated guard tower suggest that a small garrison of soldiers was based here. From an upstairs oriel window, the bishop used to bless pilgrims who gathered here on Colmán's feast day, 29 October.

The most striking feature of the site is a tenth-century round tower, 30m high. It is one of the tallest in Ireland, and leans 0.6m out of perpendicular. This is probably because it lacks deep foundations, being built on soft earth over the site of an early Christian burial ground. When the tower was restored in the late nineteenth century, skeletons were found lying oriented east to west beneath the centre of the tower and below its walls. The tower had seven timber floors, where many people could take refuge. The lower portion of the tower was found to be filled with large and small stones; above this, human bones found in a deposit of ash provided evidence of a disastrous fire. Copper fragments suggested that the monks had taken refuge in the tower, taking their precious church vessels with them. Viking raiders plundered the site in the tenth century, and the monastery was destroyed by the Normans in the thirteenth century. It was restored by the local chieftain and by Augustinian canons; its cemetery continues to be used for burial by families from the surrounding area.

# Columba

Perhaps the most outstanding of the Celtic monks, Columba (521–97) was a warrior and politician, a scholar, priest and poet who played an important role in both Irish and Scottish history. Columba, whose name means 'Dove', was born into the royal family of the northern Uí Néill, at Gartan in Donegal, and studied under a Christian bard in his mother's country of Leinster. He became a monk at an early age, and was ordained as a deacon in the monastery of Finnian at Moville. Later he was ordained a priest, and in about 556 he founded his first monastery at Derry in his family's territory, on land given to him by his tribe. He established various other communities, including that of Durrow, in central Ireland. Irish accounts of Columba relate how on a visit to his former abbot, Finnian of Moville, Columba borrowed a book from the library and secretly copied it at night. He was discovered when he had almost finished, and Finnian demanded the copy. This first recorded breach of copyright was brought to trial before the high king, who ruled in Finnian's favour.

Columba sailed to Scotland as a 'pilgrim for Christ'. As a successful warrior prince, politician and abbot, Columba may also have been invited by his relative Conall, the new King of Dalriada (or Argyll), to help him repel the Picts. Columba settled on Iona, an island 3 miles long, a mile off the western tip of the larger island of Mull. One tradition relates that Columba was given Iona by Conall, as a site for a monastery. We know a considerable amount about life in Columba's community, because in about 690 the ninth abbot of Iona, Adomnán, wrote *a Life of Columba* and preserved for us many details about the activities of the monks. The earliest surviving text of the *Life* was written on Iona by Dorbbéne, a monk who succeeded

Adomnán as abbot and died in 713. We are fortunate to possess such an early copy, written on goatskin parchment in a heavy Irish hand.

Columba lived in a hut built on planks on a small rocky mound in the monastery compound. The mound can still be seen in front of the large Benedictine abbey which was later built on the site. This may also be the 'little hill overlooking the monastery' from which, according to Adomnán, Columba gave his final blessing to the monks before his death. Adomnán describes the monks walking across the island with their farm implements on their backs to reach the sandy plain on the west side of the island where they grew their crops, using seaweed as fertiliser. He tells us of the white horse which carried the milk churns from the cow pasture, and he mentions expeditions to larger islands to fetch wood for building, since there were no trees on Iona. Adomnán pictures the monks writing manuscripts and praying in the small church, where Columba's clear voice could be heard above the others. He could also be recognised by his white cowl, or hooded cloak, for the other monks wore unbleached cowls. Plates 13 and 14 show scenes on Iona today which may not be very different from those of Columba's time.

The *Life* refers to 55 sea voyages back and forth between Iona and Ireland. Monks and pilgrims came to visit or to join the community. Those travelling from Scotland crossed the island of Mull and then shouted across the sound to Iona, for a brother to ferry them over. From his hut on planks, Columba could see them coming. On arrival, guests had their hands and feet washed. There are few remains of Iona's Celtic monastery; St Odhráin's chapel is the earliest building to survive on the island. It dates from the twelfth century and stands within what was probably the first Christian burial ground on Iona. It is named after an early monk who may have lived here before Columba's arrival. Odhráin's oratory resembles Irish chapels of the period, with a single doorway in the west wall, decorated with chevron and beak-head ornament. It was probably rebuilt as a family burial vault by Somerled, King of the Isles, who died in 1164.

In 1979, excavations were carried out in the early seventh-century boundary ditch between the little hill on which Columba's cell was built and Odhráin's cemetery. Objects were discovered which would have been in use at the end of Columba's lifetime, including heeled shoes and other leather goods, and elegant wooden bowls which had been turned on a lathe in the monastic workshops. The monks also produced fine-quality metalwork and glass ornaments. The great rectangular ramparts which surrounded the monastery can still be traced. They were constructed around the time of Columba's death; alongside them was a hedge of hawthorn and holly. The tiny chapel in front of the Benedictine abbey is built on Celtic foundations, and may mark the site of Columba's shrine. There are three elaborate high crosses and a winding path of large stones known as the 'Street of the Dead'. Chieftains were brought to Iona from the Scottish mainland for burial, and this was the track along which they were solemnly carried.

Outside the rampart, 300m to the north-east, are the remains of another Celtic cemetery, named *Cladh an Disirt* in Gaelic. It was entered through an impressive gateway framed by two large stone pillars. These supported a giant lintel, which has now fallen. The cemetery was enclosed by a wall and beside it was a hermitage,

*Iona: Gateway to the cemetery named Cladh an Disirt.*

whose superior is named in a twelfth-century list of monastic officials. There are the remains of a medieval stone chapel beside the entrance to the cemetery.

Columba lived on Iona for 35 years. He returned to Ireland in 575 after an absence of 12 years to attend an assembly of the Uí Néill clan at Druimm-Cete in Derry, as adviser to Áedán, the new king of Dalriada. The assembly agreed to Dalriada's independence from Ireland. The standing of the Irish bards was also discussed, and Columba argued in their favour. Columba returned to Ireland 10 years later to visit his own monastery at Durrow and that of Ciarán at Clonmacnoise. He died on Whitsun Eve in 597, in his monastery on Iona.

From Columba's time onwards, Iona was considered to be the centre of Celtic learning. Irish monks came to Iona to study and pray, as did Irish-trained monks from across Europe. Meanwhile, brothers from Iona played a leading part in the spread of Christianity among the Picts of eastern Scotland and the Anglo-Saxons of Northumbria. The Columban monastery of Lindisfarne was founded by Aidan, a monk from Iona, and these two communities became focal points of the Columban family, its cultural traditions and its manuscript art.

Iona suffered a number of Norse raids. In 806, during their third attack, Vikings killed 68 monks, and the remainder of the community decided to transfer to Ireland. They acquired the monastery of Kells in eastern Ireland, and left Iona, taking their belongings with them.

## Columbanus

Chief among the Irish missionaries to Europe was Columbanus (c. 540–615). He was born in Leinster, probably of a noble family, and was well educated. He was a monk in Congal's monastery of Bangor at the head of Belfast Lough in north-east Ireland until he was about 50, when he sailed to Gaul with 12 companions. He landed in Burgundy, where the king gave him a ruined Roman fort for a monastery at Annegray in the Vosges Mountains. The community grew, and Columbanus then established Fontaines and Luxeuil, which became one of the leading monasteries in Europe, sending monks as far as Bavaria.

His monks followed Celtic customs and calculated the date of Easter according to the Celtic calendar. A lengthy letter to Pope Gregory the Great survives, in which Columbanus explains his position. The Roman bishops of Gaul summoned Columbanus to a council, where he defended his views. He also challenged the royal family by refusing to bless the illegitimate sons of the new king, and in 610, together with his monks, he was taken under armed escort to Nantes to be deported back to Ireland. While waiting to set sail, he wrote a touching letter to the young monks who were left behind, urging them to make foundations, encouraging their new abbot and telling them of his sorrow at leaving them.

A storm prevented the ship from setting out, so, with some of his monks from Luxeuil, Columbanus rowed up the Rhine, hoping to settle beside Lake Constance, but he encountered further opposition and decided to cross the Alps into Italy. His companion, Gall (d. c. 630), who had come from Bangor with him, remained in Switzerland, living as a hermit. A century later a community was established on the site of Gall's hermitage, and the town of St Gall grew around it. In around 613 Columbanus settled at Bobbio in northern Italy, where he and his followers built a monastery on the site of a ruined church. He died two years later and was buried in Bobbio, while his pastoral staff was taken back across the Alps to his friend Gall in Switzerland. Due to his example, his inspiration and his pioneering achievements, Columbanus is considered to be the greatest of Ireland's missionaries to Europe.

The chapel of the Saxon palace at Cheddar in Somerset is dedicated to Columbanus, as are also, perhaps, St Columb Major, 5 miles east of Newquay in Cornwall; St Columb Minor, 2 miles east of Newquay; and Culbone, on the coast path 2 miles west-north-west of Porlock, Somerset. Cheddar is an ancient settlement at the base of a gorge, which was a route through the Mendip hills in ancient times, as we can tell from the artefacts left by cave-dwellers near the lower end of the gorge. The caves show evidence of occupation from at least 12,000 BC. In the Romano-British period, several caves in the gorge were inhabited; pottery and tools were found here and over 200 Roman coins. Where the land levels out, beside the River Yeo, a Roman villa was laid out, and long after it lay in ruins, a minster church was built on the site. This location may have been chosen because Christians had owned the villa and were buried there. King Alfred's will speaks of a community of priests at Cheddar.

Not far from the church, the Kings of Wessex Community School is the site of an early medieval settlement, and possibly a Celtic one. In 1960 Philip Rahtz discovered the remains of an Anglo-Saxon palace in the grounds of the school. The building

*Chapel of St Columbanus, Cheddar. In the foreground of the photo, markers indicate the outline of the great hall.*

was made of wood and had a thatched roof. This first timber hall was dated to the late ninth century, the very end of King Alfred's reign. According to the *Anglo-Saxon Chronicle*, the kings of Wessex met here in 942, 956 and 968. The site can be visited; outlined in the grass are the positions of a twelfth- to fourteenth-century great hall and a twelfth-century *witan*, or council chamber.

There are substantial remains of a tenth-century chapel, dedicated to Columbanus; the discovery of a single tenth-century coin helped to date the building. The chapel's dedication to an Irish missionary in Europe may be explained by intermarriage between the Saxon royal family and that of Lotharingia, a region which is now split between eastern France and western Germany. This was a region where Columbanus had worked. In the eleventh century, one of the bishops of Wells came from Lotharingia. The chapel was rebuilt in the eleventh century and again in the thirteenth, when the bishops of Wells restored both the chapel and the east hall. By then, the complex was probably no more than a royal hunting lodge with a hall, a chapel and a domestic annexe.

## Congar: see Cyngar

# Constantine

There are traditions about a Constantine who became a holy man in Brittany, Scotland, Wales and Cornwall, but they are unlikely to refer to the same person. In the sixth century, Gildas censured Constantine, King of Dumnonia (or south-western Britain) for adultery and the murder of two princes, but promised God's forgiveness if he repented. Later writers went further and described Constantine's conversion. Two places are named after Constantine in Cornwall, one near Padstow and the other 5 miles south-west of Falmouth in south-west Cornwall. This is the larger of the two villages named Constantine, situated at the head of a creek beside the estuary of Helford River. There was an early monastery here, which lasted until the eleventh century.

The author of the eleventh-century *Life of Petroc* describes a wealthy man named Constantine hunting deer at Little Petherick. Petroc interrupted the hunt, saved the stag and converted Constantine. The author was weaving local traditions into his story, for on the coast near Padstow, 3 miles north-west of Little Petherick, was St Constantine's chapel and holy well. The ancient well chapel is 3m long and 1.5m wide. The corbelled slate building has stone benches along either side and a water channel in the floor between them. There is a niche above the well at the south end.

The well was still much visited in the eighteenth century. The antiquarian William Hals says it was 'stronge built of stone and arched over; on the inner part whereof are places or seates for people to sitt and wash themselves in the stream thereof'. Over time, the well house became buried by sand dunes; it was rediscovered and excavated in 1911. The tiny chapel can be seen, protected beneath a shelter, on the golf course in Harlyn Bay. On rising ground 50m away are the ruins of Constantine church, with its tower, chancel, nave and south aisle. It was rebuilt in the fifteenth century, but suppressed in about 1540, after which the church became buried by sand. At one time it was surrounded by a graveyard and houses. Its fine Norman font of black catacleuse stone was taken 2 miles inland to its mother church of St Merryn.

*Head of an early cross in Constantine churchyard, near Falmouth.*

## Corentin

An important Breton saint, Corentin is first mentioned in a late ninth-century *Life of Winwaloe*, written by Abbot Wrdisten of Landévennec in western Brittany. Because of his holiness, local people chose him to be the first bishop of the Breton diocese of Cornouaille; he was said to have been consecrated by Martin of Tours. Quimper cathedral and five other Breton churches are dedicated to him. The Cornish village of Cury probably preserves a pet form of his name; the village is near the west coast of the Lizard, 4 miles south of Helston. There is a Celtic cross in the churchyard and a decorated Norman arch over the south door. Inside the church there is a medieval painting of Corentin dressed as a bishop with a mitre, a staff and a fish, because his thirteenth-century Breton *Life* describes him as a hermit who took a slice of the same fish each day for his meal. On a ledge, a modern wooden statue also depicts the saint.

*Statue of Corentin in Cury church.*

## Crónán of Roscrea

Crónán was an abbot and bishop of Roscrea; his father was named Odhran and his mother came from west Clare. He spent his youth in Connacht and later settled in a remote wooded marsh at Loch Cre, but found it too inhospitable, so he abandoned it and founded a monastery with a school in about 610 at Roscrea (*Ros Cre* means 'the wood of Cre') in County Tipperary. Crónán died in about 640.

Roscrea lies in southern central Ireland at the junction of the N7 and the N62; its monastery was plundered and burnt many times. The present ruins date from the twelfth century. They consist of a round tower, thought to have originally been 24m high and, across the road, the Romanesque west front of the cathedral of St Crónán. Above its round-headed doorway is the figure of a bishop, probably Crónán. The remainder of the cathedral was destroyed in 1812 to make way for the new parish church. A twelfth-century high cross stood nearby.

*The west doorway, Roscrea cathedral.*

The monastic site has been bisected by the modern road through the town. A magnificent gospel book, the *Book of Dimma*, was preserved at the monastery for centuries; its scribe, Dimma Mac Nathi, signed his name at the end of each gospel. Its cover was richly gilt in the twelfth century; it is preserved in Trinity College Library, Dublin. Roscrea was the centre of a diocese; it was later incorporated into that of Killaloe.

## Cubert

The Cornish village of Cubert may be named after a Welsh monk who also gave his name to the Welsh town of Gwbert-on-Sea, 2 miles north of Ceredigion. Cubert is 3 miles south-west of Newquay and 2 miles from the sea; other monks from Ceredigion are commemorated in nearby Cornish settlements. A farm named Lanlovey on land adjoining Cubert church suggests that this was a Celtic foundation, since the prefix *lan* is the Celtic word for a church site. An inscribed gravestone set into the outer wall of the tower indicates an early Christian presence. A Celtic cross shaft is built into the outer wall of the porch of the small, solid church. By the fourteenth century, it was believed that the parish was named after the northern saint, Cuthbert, but thirteenth-century documents name the parish saint as Cubert.

Two miles to the north-west, Cubert is honoured at a freshwater well in a sea cave, beyond the sand dunes in Holywell Bay. There are three caves, and in the furthest of these, a series of steps against the cave wall leads up to four or five shallow pools, formed by condensation dripping from the cave roof. The rock is pink and white from calcareous deposits, and the cave is accessible for only an hour each day, at low tide. In wet weather, the rocks are too slippery to climb, but in dryer conditions one can clamber past the pools into a chamber in the cave roof. In earlier times, pilgrims flocked to the well; this suggests that the sea level has altered since then as the cave is now rarely above water level. Its fresh water was good for bowel conditions and cured children's diseases. Mothers brought sick or deformed children here, and cripples left their crutches in the cave.

*St Cubert's well inside a cave, Holywell Bay.*

There is a second well in Holywell Bay, in the sand dunes. It is enclosed in a medieval chapel, with a surrounding wall. To visit it, park where the road ends. Take the track leading to the bay, but turn right through the dunes, roughly following the stream. Keep to its left bank. Enter the golf course and at once bear right, downhill. Pick up the track through a copse beside the stream. After 5 minutes' walk through the copse, the well chapel is on the left, before a flight of steps that leads up to the golf course again.

# Cwyfan

The medieval *Life of Beuno* describes him gathering a band of followers, one of whom was Cwyfan. Of the four settlements dedicated to Cwyfan, one is a chapel on an islet off the Anglesey coast at Llangwyfan. Another is at Tudweiliog on the Lleyn peninsula, where pilgrims visited his holy well in order to be cured of sore eyes, ague and warts. There is another Llangwyfan in Denbighshire. Llangwyfan on Anglesey is a tidal islet, north of Aberffraw. The island is less than an acre in area, and in summer the grass of the raised churchyard is studded with pink thrift and golden birdsfoot trefoil. The isolated rock is connected to the mainland at low tide by a causeway 200m long. The single-chambered church dates from the fourteenth to the sixteenth century, and contains some Norman stonework. The Eucharist was celebrated here, when the tide and weather allowed, until the mid nineteenth century. The priest was entitled to demand from the proprietor of Plas Llangwyfan on the mainland: a tithe of two eggs, a penny loaf, half a pint of beer and hay for his horse. The church is usually locked. To find it, take the A4080 out of Aberffraw, heading north-west for Holyhead. After a mile, turn left along a rough road into a motorbike racing area. Go through its entrance kiosk, where you can check directions. Continue along the road and fork right. Park where the road ends; Cwyfan's islet is ahead of you.

*The islet of Llangwyfan, Anglesey.*

Cwyfan is also honoured at Dyserth, 3 miles south-east of Rhyl, near the north Welsh coast, where his church is close to a high waterfall. The name Dyserth comes from the Latin word *desertum*, which means 'an empty place'. This is the western equivalent of the Greek word *eremos* or 'desert hermitage', an ancient monastic word which was used by the monks and nuns who went into the deserts of Syria, Egypt and Palestine in search of a solitary place to pray. European pilgrims were impressed by the wisdom and holiness of these Desert Mothers and Fathers, and wished to follow their example. Since there were no deserts in Britain, monks searched for a similar 'empty place' on a rocky headland or small island, or in a remote valley. Scattered across Ireland, Scotland and Wales are places named Dyserth, Dysart or *Díseart* in Irish. Each indicates an 'empty place' where a person could search for God in solitude.

Cwyfan or his unknown follower chose a magnificent location for his 'desert', within sound and sight of the waterfall's spray. The pool at its foot provided water for drinking and washing, and a place in which to immerse candidates for baptism. Watercress, valued as food by Celtic monks, grows thickly in the cold stream flowing past the church. Inside, the remains of two elaborate Celtic crosses indicate that a community continued on the site. Half a mile north-west of the church is Cwyfan's well, now dry. Until 80 years ago, people still fished for trout in the well. Fish in wells were regarded with awe and respect, and were considered to bring healing. To find the well, with the church on your right, continue along the road. Turn right at the main road. The well is soon visible in a square, stone well house, beside the road, on the right.

# Cybi

It is possible that Cybi was a sixth-century monk who travelled from Cornwall to Wales. The earliest surviving *Life of Cybi*, dating from around 1200, states that he was born in Cornwall, the son of a chieftain. Two churches in Cornwall are dedicated to him. One is at Tregony on the south coast; this was formerly a port in the tidal estuary of the River Fal. Cybi's other Cornish church is at Duloe, 4 miles south of Liskeard, on an exposed site. It was already a holy place: on the edge of the village is Cornwall's smallest stone circle, consisting of eight large white quartz stones. It may encircle a chieftain's burial mound, since a late Bronze Age burial urn was found at the base of one of the stones and a golden torc, or neck ornament, was found here.

Cybi's church stands on high ground, perhaps inside an Iron Age fort, 300m south-west of the stone circle. A massive stone font inside the church dates from early times. It is decorated with a gryphon on one side and a fish on the other, to symbolise evil and the Christian's rebirth into goodness, for the fish was an early Christian symbol for Christ. Cybi's well is half a mile east of the church, beside the road to Looe. It is set in a clump of laurels, on the opposite side of the road to West North Farm a little lower down the hill. The outer chamber of the well contains a stone bench, and inside the well's inner chamber ancient steps lead down into a pool of clear water. The well house was restored by a former rector of the church.

In Wales, Cybi has dedications at Llangibby-on-Usk, north-east of Newport; at Llangybi, north-east of Lampeter in Ceredigion, where a healing well is named after him; and at Llangybi at the neck of the Lleyn peninsula, 6 miles north-east of Pwllheli, where a remarkable early medieval well house survives. The author of Cybi's thirteenth-century *Life* tells us that Maelgwyn Gwynedd granted him land for a settlement here. At the edge of a wood in a valley 500m from the church is the most complete Celtic well house in Wales. A small rectangular room built round the well adjoins a larger room enclosing a pool fed by the spring. The pool is surrounded by a paved walk; its dry-stone walls, 6m high, and its corbelled vaulting are similar in style to those of early Irish cells. Some of its giant stones are likely to date from Cybi's time and the well house has stood untouched since at least the twelfth century. To approach the well, pilgrims used two stone causeways across the damp field. A large sacred eel lived in the well, where the patient stood barelegged: if the eel coiled itself round the patient's legs, it was believed that a cure would follow.

The spring water possesses mineral properties and cured a wide variety of illnesses. A register of cures made in 1766 describes how a man who had been blind for 30 years bathed his eyes for three consecutive weeks and recovered his sight. In the eighteenth century, seven people were cured of blindness caused by smallpox. The lame came to Llangybi on crutches or were wheeled to the well in barrows. When they were cured, they gratefully left their crutches and barrows around the well, where they were noted by an observer in the early eighteenth century. Water was carried away in casks and bottles for use as medicine. A party of smugglers returning from a night's work with casks of spirits explained when challenged by an excise officer that the casks contained water from Ffynnon Gybi! Until the eighteenth century, the church contained a chest, Cyff Cybi, for thank offerings from pilgrims cured at the well.

According to Cybi's *Life*, Maelgwyn Gwynedd also gave him permission to build a church at Caergybi on the small island of Holyhead, which is connected to Anglesey by a causeway. A chieftain, on conversion to Christianity,

*Early well house, Llangybi, Lleyn peninsula.*

often handed over part of his fortified homestead to the Church. Maelgwyn gave Cybi a late third-century Roman coastal fort, and the church sits neatly inside it, well protected by its Roman enclosure wall with towers at each corner. Inside the south corner of the fort is *Eglwys-y-Bedd*, or 'the church of the grave', where Cybi was said to have been buried; the chapel over his tomb dates from the fourteenth century. The large medieval parish church dates from the thirteenth century. It was rebuilt in the late fifteenth and early sixteenth centuries; its elaborate porch contains fine carved stonework and a fan-vaulted roof. The whole complex lies near the centre of old Holyhead.

## Cyngar

Congresbury in Somerset is named after this saint, who may have been a missionary from Wales. Congresbury is first mentioned in Asser's *Life of Alfred* as a derelict Celtic monastery which Alfred assigned to Asser, bishop of Crediton. Cyngar's shrine in Congresbury church was a centre of pilgrimage throughout medieval times. The improbable *Life of Cyngar* tells of a dream in which a wild boar shows Cyngar where he should live. On waking, he sees a boar in a reed bed and builds an oratory on the site. A wild boar features in a number of Celtic saints' *Lives*, such as those of Cadoc and Ciarán of Saighir: often a white sow indicates where the monk's chief monastery should be built. Swineherds lived on the edge of settlements, where a monk could combine solitude with accessibility to local people. Medieval Christians familiar with the classics would recall that a huge white sow showed Ascanius where to found the great city of Alba Longa, the forerunner of Rome.

Cyngar may have been associated with the nearby hill fort of Cadbury, three-quarters of a mile to the north; this is one of five camps in the south-west to be named 'Cadbury' or 'Cada's fort'. It was probably occupied by members of the Dobunni tribe, who were based in the Cotswolds. The fort was abandoned during the Roman occupation, from AD 43 to 410, when the lowland around it was under stable Roman administration, as the region grew and flourished. However, the hill fort gained a new lease of life and was reoccupied from around AD 410 until 700. Perhaps it was now no longer safe to live in the lowlands below the fort.

Cadbury camp is the only fortress in the region to have been lived in again after the departure of the Romans. Amphorae were found here, still imported from Mediterranean lands, as they had been in Roman times. The people living here were wealthy: the fort has produced Britain's second-largest collection of fragments of early medieval glass. There were at least 60 vessels; the only site to have produced more is the monastery of Whithorn in south-west Scotland, which yielded pieces of some 80 vessels. It is possible that the monk Cyngar lived near the people in the fort, for on the adjacent hilltop of Henley Hill at Yatton is what appears to have been an early Christian cemetery. There had been a Roman temple here which fell into ruin in the third century, and later, perhaps in the sixth century, between 50 and 100 Christian graves were dug through the site. Unfortunately, the site has now been quarried away.

'Congar's Walking Stick' in Congresbury churchyard.

In Saxon times, the settlement of Congresbury grew alongside the River Yeo which flows at the foot of the fort, a mile to the south-west. Here there was a minster church and a monastery. The large oblong site of 10 acres is bounded by deep ditches and probably dates from the seventh century. There was a second church within the enclosure, dedicated to St Michael. Since the Archangel Michael is associated with the souls of the dead, this was probably a mortuary chapel.

Eleventh- and fourteenth-century pilgrim guides describe Cyngar's body enshrined in the church. In 1996, in the floor of a barn at Brinsea near Congresbury, stones were discovered which had formed part of Cyngar's eleventh-century shrine, including a piece of one of its corner pillars. It would have been a substantial monument, over 2m high. Two sculptured figures depict Christ and a tonsured saint, perhaps St Peter. A large torso fragment may have come from a statue of Cyngar. The sculptures are now in Taunton Museum. The shrine probably stood near or behind the high altar of the minster church. Next to the church there is a fine thirteenth-century priests' house, built to accommodate the clerics who ministered to the pilgrims visiting the shrine.

Cyngar's cult may have waned, for in 1217–18 the church was rebuilt and rededicated to St Andrew. The great east window was constructed at this time. St Cyngar's shrine was now seen to be in the way, and his relics were relegated to a side chapel off the south aisle, where the arched recess of his tomb can still be seen. Some of the stone foundations of his shrine were reused in the new east wall of the church, which was rebuilt yet again in the fourteenth and fifteenth centuries. In the churchyard, an ancient yew stump inside a beech tree is still known as 'Congar's Walking Stick'. Cyngar was said to have planted his staff here, where it took root, and this miracle persuaded the Saxon King Ine of Wessex to grant him land for a monastery. Even today, yew is a traditional wood for carving walking sticks.

# David

The patron saint of Wales, David (d. c. 589) lived and worked in what is now Pembrokeshire. Most of our knowledge about him comes from a *Life of David* written in about 1095 by a Norman cleric named Rhigyfarch, whose father had been bishop of St David's for 10 years. According to his *Life*, David's father was Sant, King of Ceredigion, and his mother was named Non. David rose to a position of leadership at the synod of Brefi (c. 545), which appears to have been a religious tribal gathering to refute the heretical teachings of Pelagius. This British theologian taught that people could reach heaven by their own efforts, without the help of God's grace. His emphasis on personal responsibility appealed to British chieftains, with their strong sense of self-reliance. The village of Llanddewi Brefi is 7 miles north-east of Lampeter; its name means 'David's church beside the River Brefi'.

Brefi was a natural place for an assembly: three Roman roads converge nearby, and continued in use long after the Romans departed, although by the mid sixth century they were probably becoming overgrown. At the synod, no one could make their voice heard over such a large crowd. David was a clear, convincing speaker, and was brought from nearby to address the gathering. When David's biographer, Rhigyfarch, relates this detail, Welsh readers would recall that a victorious bard could silence his opponents, just as only David could quieten the crowd and convince them of the errors of Pelagius. From then onwards, David apparently went about bareheaded and barefoot, carrying a bell which he named *bangu*, or 'dear, loud one'. He wore rough clothes and carried a large branch rather than a crosier.

Inside Llanddewi Brefi church there is a fine collection of early gravestones dating from the seventh to the tenth centuries. One is inscribed to Cenlisimus, a ninth-century abbot. Another commemorates Dumelus, a name of Irish form, which indicates that monks moved north across the River Teifi from Dyfed – a kingdom of Irish settlers. Set into the outer wall of the church are two fragments of an inscription dating from the fifth, sixth or seventh century, which may be the first surviving reference to David. The antiquarian Edward Lhuyd examined the complete stone, and concluded in 1722 that it read: 'Here lies Idnert, the son of James, who was killed while defending the church of holy David from pillage.' The fragments can be seen in the west wall of the church, on the north side.

David established a monastery on the Pembrokeshire coast, around which developed the later town of St David's. He chose a site in the narrow valley of the River Alun, hidden from pirates by a bend in the river. In his eleventh-century *Life of David*, Rhigyfarch relates that the land belonged to an Irish chieftain named Baia, who occupied an earlier hill fort above the site. Baia and his wife noticed smoke rising from the monks' settlement and challenged David in various ways, until Baia was killed by another Irish raider named Liski, who arrived in the night.

Rhigyfarch draws on an early source to describe how the monks spent their days in hard physical labour, followed by reading, writing and praying. In the evening they gathered in the church for vespers, after which they prayed silently until night fell; only then would they eat a simple meal together. The brothers returned to the chapel to pray for another few hours. After a short night's sleep, they woke at

*Early gravestones, Llanddewi Brefi. That on the right commemorates Dumelus.*

cock-crow to sing matins and to 'spend the rest of the night until morning without sleep'. This harsh pattern of life may reflect the influence of the Irish *Céli Dé* (or 'Servants of God'). This was a movement of monks who urged a return to a stricter lifestyle and a more austere diet.

Anyone seeking to join the community was to be kept waiting outside the door for ten days, to test his desire for monastic life. The candidate was then welcomed by the doorkeeper, and put to work alongside the monks for many months, 'until the natural stubbornness of his heart was broken'. When the abbot judged that he was well prepared, the novice was eventually invited to join the community. This unusually severe style of life was designed to imitate that of the monks of the Near Eastern deserts.

St David's cathedral was rebuilt in 1275, largely from offerings at his shrine. The English Kings William I and Henry II made the long journey to the cathedral. During William the Conqueror's visit in 1081, the Welsh princes probably appealed to the king to uphold the Welsh Church against the increasing power of Rome. A modern oak casket in the cathedral was thought to contain relics of David and of a hermit named Justinian, who lived on nearby Ramsey Island and became a friend of David. However, radiocarbon dating in 2002 established that the bones in the casket are likely to be only 700 years old; David's relics were probably destroyed at the Reformation. They would have been contained in the thirteenth-century stone shrine which still survives; it formerly had a wooden canopy and painted panels depicting saints David, Patrick and Denis. The shrine contains apertures in which pilgrims' offerings could be placed; it stood in the sanctuary, before the high altar. David's early followers may have worked in Cornwall and Brittany. Nine churches in Cornwall were named after him.

# Déclán

Déclán was one of the monks who worked in south-east Ireland in the early fifth century before the arrival of Patrick. His *Life* relates that he came from the royal house of the Déisi, a tribe who had been expelled from Tara in Meath. Déclán was born in Lismore and established a monastery 20 miles further south, on the coast at Ardmore, in about 416. According to his twelfth-century *Life*, the area was mainly pagan at Déclán's birth, but a priest named Colmán came to his home, introduced his parents to Christianity and baptised Déclán. He went abroad to study and returned with his monk's bell and staff. He preached, baptised and built churches among the Déisi. When he went further afield and preached to King Aongus of Cashel, the king refused baptism, since the clan of Aongus were not on good terms with the Déisi.

Déclán founded a monastery at Ardmore on the south coast of Ireland, halfway between Cork and Waterford. *Ard mór* means 'great height', and Déclán chose a site on fertile high ground overlooking a sandy bay. The headland may then have been an island in the mouth of the River Blackwater, before it burst its banks in 803 and made a new channel through Youghal Bay.

The ruined cathedral at Ardmore dates from the ninth century. In the chancel, two ogham-inscribed grave markers date from near to Déclán's lifetime. By the twelfth century, when Déclán's *Life* came to be written, little was known about his work, and the adventures recounted in his biography may have little basis in fact. However, there were traditions about Déclán's love of solitude and his choice of a 'desert' or place of retreat on the headland 800m beyond the monastery. His hermitage was here, in a sheltered spot beside a spring. In old age, he was said to have moved out of the monastic 'city' in order to come and live here. Déclán's

*Déclán's Desert, Ardmore.*

Desert is still a peaceful place surrounded by trees. In the early morning one can look out across the sparkling sea and watch fishermen in the bay, far below. There are remains of a large ruined church; its east end dates from the fourteenth century, but its west end is earlier.

West of the ruined church is Déclán's holy well. Two small doorways lead down to the spring, where it is possible to bathe. The well house is capped with two late-medieval crosses, each bearing a figure of Christ. The well was restored in 1798 and again in 1951. It is visited by countless people, particularly during the week nearest to Déclán's feast day, 24 July. Until the late 1940s, pilgrims came to spend all night in a prayer vigil at the well. Between the desert and the monastic city, Déclán's Stone is also visited by pilgrims. This is a large erratic boulder which balances on two smaller rocks, and is held to cure rheumatism if one crawls beneath it. In any case, the act of doing so loosens stiff joints!

An account from around 1840 describes the scene on Déclán's feast day:

> The crowd then formed a long line winding up the narrow path that leads along the mountain's brow to St Déclán's chapel ... The scenery was beautiful as we looked over the precipitous cliffs across the bay of Ardmore. On the brink stands the remnant of a chapel, said to be the first built in Ireland. On entering the gate, on your right is the well St Déclán blessed. Then they knelt down and said their prayers ... At twenty different periods, I counted people as they passed. They averaged fifty-five a minute, which gives a total of fifteen thousand persons.

The twelfth-century *Life of Déclán* relates that when he sensed death approaching, he returned from his hermitage to the community, to die among his brother monks. We read:

> When Déclán realised that his last days were at hand, he called for Mac Liag from the eastern Déisi, in order to receive the last sacraments from him. He foreknew the day of his death, and asked to be brought back to his own [monastic] city ... Mac Liag gave him the last sacraments. He blessed all his people, and when he died, he was buried with honour in the tomb which he had already chosen.

The chapel of Déclán's grave is the oldest building of the monastery, although it was restored in the eighteenth century. It is a small rectangular oratory, on what may be eighth-century foundations, on the hillside at the edge of the site where the land slopes down to the sea. Large stone blocks form the lower courses of its walls; its projecting pillars, or *antae*, would have supported the roof timbers. Generations of Christians have scooped out earth from Déclán's grave inside the chapel, since it is believed to protect from disease.

The round tower and the ruined west end of the cathedral at Ardmore date from the twelfth century. A number of fine but badly weathered Romanesque reliefs have been reassembled and set into the cathedral's west wall; they depict Adam and Eve, the adoration of the infant Christ by the three wise men and other scenes. The round tower was one of the latest to be built in Ireland. Beautifully proportioned, it rises to a height of 29m. Its four tapering storeys are separated by projecting string courses, each resembling a rope. The round-arched doorway is 4m above ground level, so that defenders could enter by ladder and pull it in after them, to prevent its use by attackers. An unusual feature of the tower is that inside are projecting stones carved with grotesque heads.

Towers may have served as lookout posts and landmarks, and guides for sailors and travellers on land. Books, chalices and shrines could be safely stored here, and monks could take refuge in the tower. This one was so strong that it withstood an attack with cannon fire when it was held by the Confederates in 1642, at a time when the native Catholic population struggled against their English Protestant overlords and Oliver Cromwell ruthlessly suppressed the Irish Rebellion. The elegant tower now dominates a peaceful landscape once more.

## Decuman

Decuman is the patron saint of the small settlement at St Decumans, a mile south-west of Watchet on the north Somerset coast. He is thought to have been a sixth-century Welsh monk, possibly from Brecon. He may have given his name to a monastery at Roscrowther (formerly named Llanddegyman) in Pembrokeshire; this community was of some significance, since it is named in *The Laws of Howel the Good* as one of the 'seven bishop houses in Dyved', alongside the great monasteries of St David's, Llandeilo Fawr and others.

Decuman's name suggests that he was a Romanised Briton, since *Decumanus* is Latin for 'tenth'.

Decuman's fifteenth-century *Life* was probably written at Wells cathedral, to which St Decumans belonged. It relates that he lived as a hermit near Dunster, and was murdered one day while at prayer. Like St Nectan and others, after being beheaded, he picked up his head and walked to the spring which flows 50m north-west of the church, where his life blood conferred healing properties on the water. In Celtic thought, the head, rather than the heart, was regarded as the source of life. These stories were told to demonstrate the saint's power over death.

*Semi-circular pool, St Decuman's well.*

The spring is down a lane below the church, on the steeply sloping hillside. It is covered by a circular well house, and a little lower down the slope the water flows into two semi-circular basins before going underground. A record from around 1100 states: 'The fountain of St Decumanus is sweet, healthful, and necessary to the inhabitants for drinking purposes.' A Byzantine coin from the mint of Constantinople was found in 'St Decuman's Garden', which may have been the area around the well. The coin was a *follis* of Justinian I (540–41); it is more likely to have been used as jewellery than as money. St Decumans church tower is a landmark visible from some distance, both from the sea and over land. The church at St Decumans was of some importance in Saxon times; it was located on the royal estate of Williton, where it had a dependant chapel in about 1175. In 1190 St Decumans was given to Wells cathedral; the present church dates from the late thirteenth century.

# Deifor

Three miles north-east of Denbigh in north Wales, St Deifor's church of Bodfari features in the twelfth-century *Legend of Winifred*. She is said to have left Holywell with a group of nuns and travelled inland, first to Bodfari, where they stayed with a monk named Deifor, and eventually to Gwytherin. The name Bodfari means 'dwelling (or *bod*) of Deifor'. His church is on a hillside above the Roman road from Chester to Caerhun, which

was a fort guarding the River Conwy. There was a Roman posting station at Bodfari and a small settlement. The Normans rededicated Deifor's church to St Stephen. Huge buttresses anchor the medieval church into the hillside. The key to the church can be obtained from the post office across the road.

A thirteenth-century manuscript mentions Deifor's well, 100m down the road from the church, opposite the site of the Roman station. The well can be seen within a concrete surround beside the road. Even after the Reformation, villagers went in procession from the church down to the well, where the Litany, the Ten Commandments, the Epistle and

*Bodfari church, built into the hillside.*

Gospel were read. The poorest person in the parish offered a chicken after walking nine times round the well, a cock for a boy or a pullet for a girl. Children were also 'dipped to the neck at three of its corners, to prevent their crying at night'.

## Deiniol

The sixth-century Welsh monk bishop Deiniol, or Daniel in English, was said to be a descendant of a northern British chieftain. His father, Dunawd, established a great monastery at Bangor-is-y-Coed beside the River Dee, 4 miles south-east of Wrexham. Deiniol spent time here as a monk, and a number of churches in the surrounding area are dedicated to him. Deiniol left his father's community to found one of his own. He travelled west through the mountains and established Bangor beside the Menai Strait on land given to him by Maelgwyn, Prince of Gwynedd, marking out the new site by driving posts into the ground and weaving branches between them. The noun *bangor* means 'the binding part of a wattle fence', and the monastery of Bangor beside the Menai Strait took its name from its surrounding palisade, as did Deiniol's father's foundation.

Deiniol's community was destroyed by Vikings in 1073. All that now survives are pieces of some ninth- or tenth-century stone crosses carved with geometric designs. They can be seen in the cathedral, which became the centre of one of Britain's earliest dioceses. Deiniol's son gave his name to a small settlement across the Menai Strait in Anglesey, Llanddaniel Fab (or 'church of Daniel the Younger'). Unlike Deiniol's magnificent fourteenth-century cathedral, his son's church is hidden behind a row of houses in the village that bears his name.

*Church of Llanddaniel Fab, Anglesey.*

# Derfel

A sixth-century missionary, possibly of Breton origin, Derfel Gadarn ('the Mighty') was said to have been a soldier before becoming a hermit at Llandderfel in mid Wales. Four miles east-north-east of Bala, Llandderfel is set on a valley slope, near the headwaters of the River Dee. Until the Reformation there was an ancient wooden statue in the church of Derfel mounted on a horse or possibly a red deer stag. Thomas Cromwell, whom King Henry VIII made responsible for the confiscation of church property, sent agents throughout Britain to seize goods and 'abolish Popish practices'. There is a record of Cromwell's agent in Wales writing to his master in 1538 for instructions about Derfel's statue, because 'the people have so much trust in him that they come daily on pilgrimage to him with cows or horses or money, to the number of five or six hundred on April 5th' (Derfel's feast day). Cromwell had the statue of Derfel brought to London to be burnt at Smithfield, but the rider's wooden mount can still be seen in the church porch. It stood in the chancel beside the communion table until 1730, when the rural dean, who disliked the presence of images in church, removed it and sawed off half of the animal's head.

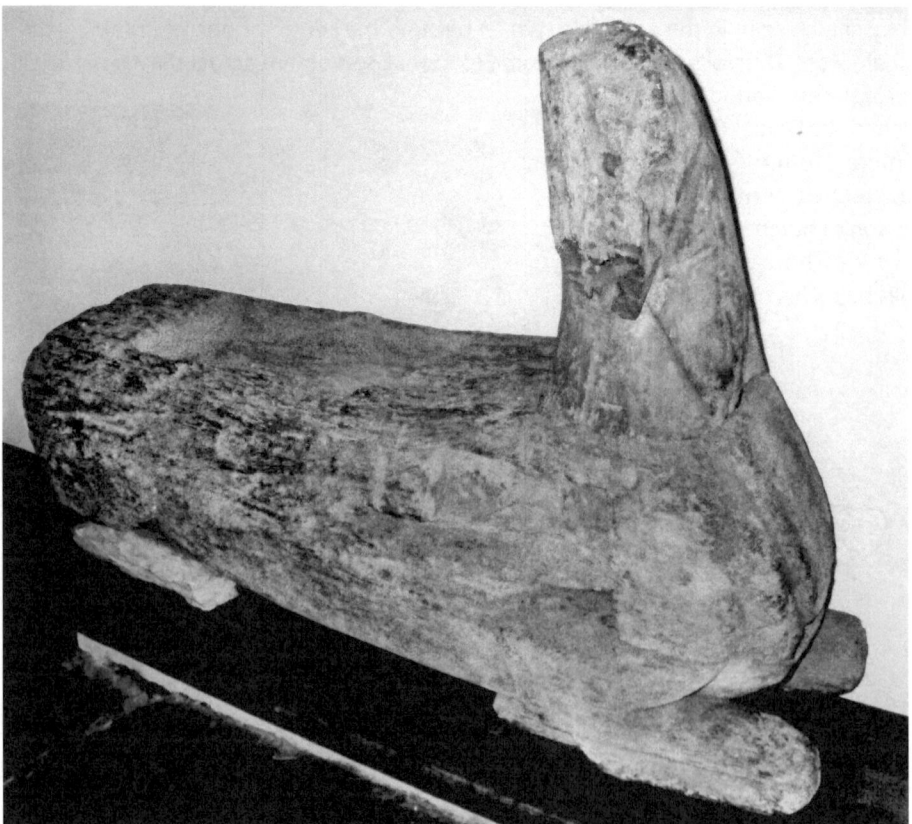

*Derfel's wooden horse, Llandderfel.*

The wooden horse was still brought out each Easter Tuesday around the time of Derfel's feast, and carried in procession to the Wake Field, where it was fixed to a pole for children to ride. Despite its damage through the centuries, the recumbent beast retains considerable character, with its deep eye sockets and most of its head half-turned over its right shoulder. The small church has a magnificent oak rood screen, carved in about 1500. Llandderfel was sufficiently remote to remain a centre for Catholic worship; the last Mass in north Wales until recent times was celebrated here. The church is on a rise, near the end of the village. The key can be obtained from the former vicarage, now a nursing home, up the road, across from the church.

## Docco

Docco established a monastery at Llandough, in south-east Wales, and St Kew, 5 miles north-east of Wadebridge near the north Cornish coast, appears to have been its daughter house; it was then known as Landocco, or 'the church of Docco'. Mentioned in the seventh-century *Life of Samson*, it is the earliest named Cornish monastery. This is where, according to his seventh-century *Life*, St Samson hoped to stay with his companions, but was dissuaded from doing so by its monks, apparently because they had grown lax, and did not want to incur Bishop Samson's disapproval.

A bilingual grave marker has survived from its cemetery: a rounded pillow stone which marked the head of a grave. The mason carved the name of the dead man in Latin, writing IUSTI, which means '[the stone of] Justus', and enclosed the name within a roughly carved cartouche. Along the edge of the gravestone, the sculptor inscribed the man's name in Irish ogham, a stroke alphabet which was used frequently in south-east Ireland, but rarely in Cornwall. The pillow stone can be seen inside the church, in a corner to the left of the door.

*Pillar stone, inscribed IUSTI, St Kew.*

There is some medieval stained glass in the windows and a tall Celtic cross in the churchyard. A holy well in the grounds of Trescobel, the former vicarage, was probably the monks' water supply. It was frequently visited by pilgrims; its well house was restored in 1890. To visit the well, park beside the church; with the church and a telephone kiosk to your left, walk along the road out of the village for 5 minutes, following the high wall of the former vicarage. With permission, walk round to the front of the house and along the drive to the gate. The well is just inside the front gate, along a path to the right.

## Dubricius (Dyfrig)

An important Romano-British monk bishop, Dubricius (d. c. 550), has a number of dedications in Hereford and Gwent. His mother was a chieftain's daughter from the small territory of Erging in Herefordshire. He was said to have been born at Madley, near Hereford. The seventh-century *Life of Samson* presents Dubricius as a prominent figure among the Christians of south Wales. It relates that Dubricius appointed Samson as abbot of the community on Caldey Island, a daughter house of the famous monastery at Llanilltud Fawr (Llantwit Major). His consecration as a bishop is described, as is his ordination of Samson as a deacon.

Caldey Island is 3 miles south of Tenby, at the south-western point of Cardigan Bay. In Celtic times, the island was known as Ynys Pyr, after its first abbot. The *Life of Samson* describes Pyr's undignified death: walking back to his cell one night, the drunken abbot fell into the monastery's well and drowned. Dubricius had authority over the community and appointed Samson as abbot to replace Pyr. There are many caves around the island's coastline; the monks may have lived in these and in wattle huts clustered around a church near the spring, which still supplies the island with abundant fresh water.

Near the centre of the island is St Illtud's church and the remains of a Norman priory, with a distinctive stone watchtower. The present church with its floor of cobblestones dates from the

*St Illtud's church, with its cobbled floor, Caldey Island.*

thirteenth and fourteenth centuries. Located against the south wall of the nave is a grave slab inscribed in ogham with what may read *'Magl Dubr ...'* or '[the stone of] the tonsured servant of Dubricius'. Below that is an early Latin inscription which may be translated as: '... And I have provided it with a cross. I ask all who walk in this place to pray for the soul of Cadwgan.'

Writing in about 1811, the antiquarian Fenton says that the stone was dug up in the ruins of the priory 'many years ago'. Ynys Pyr was a foundation of some significance: a fragment of sixth-century pottery from the eastern Mediterranean and the base of a seventh-century jar from Gaul were found near the tiny parish church of St David, which may be built on foundations dating from Celtic times; its site was then just above the high-water mark. Linked with the monastery was a community of nuns on St Margaret's Island, which adjoins Caldey. At that time it was possible to walk across low-lying marsh to St Margaret's Island from the mainland at Penally. There are frequent daily boat crossings to Caldey Island from Tenby on weekdays throughout the year; the journey takes about 20 minutes. There are Saturday sailings from mid May to mid September, but none on Sundays. This enables the Cistercian monks who now live on the island to enjoy its tranquillity once a week. At high tide, boats leave from Tenby harbour; at low water they depart from the landing stage on Castle Beach. Tickets can be obtained from the Caldey Island kiosk at the top of Tenby harbour.

Dubricius' chief monastery was at Hentland, near Ross-on-Wye. The name Hentland comes from the Welsh *hen llan* ('old, or former, church'), a name which often describes a church restored after a period of disuse. Hentland is at the end of a road half a mile south of Kynaston, 4 miles west-north-west of Ross-on-Wye. There was a Roman building here before the time of Dubricius. Part of the nave of the church dates from 1050, but most of the building is thirteenth century. In the churchyard is a thirteenth-century lantern cross; its worn carvings include a crucifixion scene and the figure of a bishop, presumably Dubricius.

The twelfth-century *Book of Llandaff* describes Dubricius building a dwelling and a chapel dedicated to the Trinity at Moccas, 8 miles east of Hay-on-Wye. Its name comes from *Mochros*, meaning 'the place of pigs'; its Trinitarian dedication may indicate that the text was composed in an Anglo-Norman context. A white boar appears as a messenger from God, to show Dubricius the place where he is to build. In medieval hagiography, other Celtic saints who were shown the site of their chief monastery by a wild boar were Illtud and Cadoc, Brynach of Nevern, Cyngar, Kentigern, Paul Aurelian and Ciarán of Saighir.

Dubricius is said to have retired to Bardsey Island in old age, and to have died there. His cult was taken further afield: the church of Porlock on the north Somerset coast was at some point dedicated to him, for the church is called 'ecclesia S. Dubricii' in the foundation deed of the Harrington chantry chapel in 1476. The yew tree in the churchyard dates from early times. Inside the church are two pieces of a pre-Norman cross, which is the earliest stone carving in west Somerset. The church was formerly closer to the sea, which has now receded. Its stocky tower, perhaps dating from the thirteenth century, may have had a light on top of its spire to guide boats into the harbour.

# Eilian

Eilian was a monk from Anglesey who was said to have cured Maelgwyn Gwynedd's father, Cadwallon, of blindness. In return for being cured, Cadwallon gave Eilian a grant of land to build a church at what was later named Llaneilian. According to the story, Cadwallon gave him as much land as his tame doe could cross in a day, but a rich person's greyhound killed the doe and was cursed by Eilian. Until the mid nineteenth century, pilgrims came from all parts of north Wales to Eilian's well near the shore for a blessing on cattle and corn, and for the cure of ague, fits, scrofula and other diseases; their offerings were placed in a chest in the church. Eilian's well was also visited in order to curse one's enemies, as Eilian was said to have done.

Llaneilian is a village on the north-east coast of Anglesey, a mile east of Amlwch. Eilian's shrine still survives; it is built of plain panelled wood. The church dates from the fifteenth century, with a fourteenth-century chancel, from which a stone passage leads to Eilian's chapel. This is a small room, 4.5m by 3.5m. Eilian's shrine is here; formerly, pilgrims used to crawl through it as they prayed for healing. There is a fine fifteenth-century oak rood screen in the chancel. A feature of the church is its twelfth-century spire; there is a medieval preaching cross in the churchyard.

*Llaneilian: fifteenth-century oak rood screen.*

# Endellion

Described as one of the 12 daughters of Brychan, we first hear of Endellion in the twelfth-century *Life of Nectan*, written at Hartland abbey in north Devon. The church of St Endellion is near the north Cornish coast. In the early seventeenth century, the antiquarian Nicholas Roscarrock, who lived in the parish, believed that Endellion lived at Trentinny, a farm half a mile south of the church. Two nearby holy wells are also named after her.

The village of St Endellion is 1½ miles from the north Cornish coast, and 8 miles north of Wadebridge; it is one of a cluster of parishes named after the sons, or more often the daughters, of Brychan. Twenty early Christian graves were discovered near the church, on the opposite side of the B3314. Not far away, a sixth-century pillar stone, 1.5m high, stands at the first crossroads on the minor road from St Endellion church to Portquin. Coincidentally, it is dedicated to a Christian named Brychan (whose name means 'Little Badger'). Beneath a *chi-rho* symbol for Christ, its worn inscription reads in translation: 'Brocagnus lies here, the son of Nadottus.' The dead man would not have been Endellion's father, but the inscription indicates that the name Brychan was current in early times.

By the thirteenth century, St Endellion housed a college of priests. The church contains a Norman font and a fine barrel roof. The present church dates from the fifteenth century and is built of moor stone; the tower, however, was constructed of stone from Lundy Island, 40 miles to the north. Lundy is visible from the churchyard on a clear day. Endellion's shrine survives at the east end of the south aisle of the church. It was carved of black catacleuse stone in the fourteenth century. It contains eight deep niches; the tomb now serves as an altar.

*St Endellion's shrine, in her church.*

# Euny

Euny was a widely revered Cornish saint venerated in at least five places in western Cornwall; his earliest cult centre was probably Lelant, where he was said to be buried. He is also linked with Crowan, Merther Euny, Redruth and Chapel Euny in Sancreed. He may have been a British monk, although in 1478 William of Worcester heard that he was an Irishman, the brother of Erth and Ia. In the sixteenth century, boys were named Euny, particularly in Redruth.

A well near Sancreed church, 4 miles west of Penzance, is named after Euny. Sancreed is a Celtic foundation with a circular churchyard where there is a fine tenth-century cross inscribed by the sculptor with his name, Runhol. Spelling was evidently less important at this time, since the carver spelt his name as RUNHO at Sancreed and as RUHOL on the cross now in Lanherne. An early inscribed stone in Sancreed churchyard was turned upside down in the thirteenth century and carved to resemble the Runhol cross.

Euny's holy well is 300m south-west of the church. To find it, cross the road which runs past the church and take the footpath signed 'holy well'. A small working garage is ahead of you. As you pass it you will see a stile to the right, beside a gate. Climb the stile and continue to walk along the lane for 5 minutes, past a concrete pump house. Wellingtons are useful here, where the ground floods. The well is now ahead of you, in an enclosure, down a steep flight of nine granite steps. Beside the well is an ancient thorn bush hung with clouties, or rags which represent prayers. Close by are the walls of a small rectangular chapel. Nearby, massive granite blocks form the wall of an earlier building, perhaps a monk's cell.

Another nearby well and a ruined chapel are named after Euny at the ancient British village of Carn Euny, 2 miles west of Sancreed, which was occupied from the fifth century BC to the fourth century AD. By then it consisted of three interlocking courtyard houses, with a well-preserved *fougou*, which may have been used for storage and for hiding underground, if necessary. The copious well of Chapel Euny, half a mile away,

*St Euny's well, Sancreed.*

was probably the water supply for this Romano-British village. There are actually two wells and the remains of a ruined chapel. To find the twin wells, park as if visiting Carn Euny. Consult the site plan and follow the longer track, labelled 'Route 2, 450 metres'. Where the track veers to the right for Carn Euny, continue instead for a short distance up the hill and take the muddy track to the left. After 5 minutes, you will see the wells, surrounded by giant stone slabs. An ancient thorn tree, now adorned with clouties, is down a path to the left, beside the stream flowing from the wells.

## Féchín

Féchín was a holy man from Sligo who travelled widely in Ireland; his first foundation was at Fore in Westmeath. He later established other communities, including one at Cong, beside Lough Corrib, from which a fine cross survives. Carved in about 1123, the processional cross is made of oak decorated with metal filigree, and was designed to enclose a relic of the cross of Christ at its centre. The earliest manuscript of Féchín's *Life* comes from his island settlement of Ard Oilean, off the coast of Connemara. There are monastic ruins at most of Féchín's foundations, a few dating from his lifetime. Féchín died of the yellow plague in the 660s. His followers took his cult to Scotland, where the monastery of St Vigeans at Arbroath near the Fife coast is named after him.

The first monastery established by Féchín was on a hillside at Fore. The site is 2½ miles east of Castlepollard and 20 miles west of Navan. In the tenth century, a simple rectangular church was built on the hillside. Its west doorway is capped with a giant lintel decorated with a plain carved cross within a circle. A small graveyard surrounds the church; it contains a high cross and a tower house known as the Anchorite's Cell, with a nineteenth-century mausoleum built onto it. The monastery was a bishopric until the twelfth century, when the Normans built a large Benedictine abbey in the valley below, and life probably ended at Féchín's foundation. The fortress-like ruins of the abbey include a church, two tower houses, part of a cloister, domestic buildings and a circular dovecote. Further off in the fields are two gates, which are remains of the old town walls.

Between the Celtic monastery and the Benedictine abbey, a ruined mill is said to stand on the site of one built by Féchín. It is fed by underground streams from Lough Lene, a mile away on the far side of the mountain. The rivulets emerge from the hillside and flow into a triangular millpond before continuing through the mill. Between the mill and the Benedictine abbey, beneath an ancient ash tree, is Féchín's holy well. It is a triangular structure, its walls formed by three great stone slabs. The well is named *Doaghféighín*, or Féchín's Vat. It is now dry, but formerly contained water in which Féchín was said to have knelt in prayer. Delicate children were immersed in the water to be cured through Féchín's intercession. Gnarled roots of the ash tree are now entwined with the stones of Féchín's Vat. Clouties are tied to the tree, as mute prayers for healing.

Féchín's church of Kilboglashy is 4 miles south-west of Sligo at the head of Ballysadare Bay, where the river enters the sea. The site is 750m north-north-west

West doorway of Féchin's church, Fore.

of Ballysadare, on the west bank of the river. To find it, take the N59 westwards from Ballysadare, signed Ballina. After crossing the river, pass the first shops, continue for 20m and turn right. When the surfaced road veers left, continue straight on along an unsurfaced track. Follow this for 50m to the church, which is on the right.

The seventh-century church is known as *Teampall Mór Féchín* (or 'Féchín's great church'). It is located on the left bank of the river, overlooking a waterfall, and is now partly covered with ivy. The oldest feature of the building is the western gable and a section of the adjoining north wall. The church is 10m by 20m, and has been rebuilt a number of times. The present structure dates from the thirteenth century and incorporates twelfth-century stonework. A Romanesque doorway has been inserted into the south wall; it is decorated with carved heads. A tympanum, or decorated space above the entrance arch, may have adorned what is now a plain surface. A further 250m to the west is a fifteenth-century Augustinian church, now almost buried beneath the debris from a quarry.

# Fergus

The *Aberdeen Breviary* (1507) relates that Fergus was an early eighth-century bishop who worked as a missionary in northern and eastern Scotland, where he has many dedications. He was probably a native Pict who studied in Ireland and returned to Angus. Fergus may be the *Fergustus episcopus Scotiae Pictus* ('Fergus the Pict, bishop of Scotland') who is recorded as taking part in the Council of Rome in 721. This council condemned irregular marriages of various kinds, sorcerers and clerics who grew their hair long in the Celtic tradition.

Fergus is said to have settled at Glamis, 10 miles north of Dundee. His church is close to a pre-Christian standing stone; the cup marks at its base indicate its ancient origin. The great stone was subsequently Christianised: on one side is an interlaced cross, flanked by warriors fighting with hand axes and other symbols; on the other side are Pictish carvings of a snake, a salmon and a mirror. Fergus was said to have

*Hunter and hounds chase a stag, cross slab, Eassie.*

lived in a cave beside a holy well that flows into Glamis Burn. The cave collapsed in the nineteenth century.

There are fragments of three more Pictish cross slabs dating from the eighth and ninth centuries inside the church. A fourth stone from the same period can be seen north of the track leading south from the A94 just east of Glamis. On the front is a cross decorated with interlace and key patterns. An angel and a bird-headed man flank the upper arms of the cross, while two deer and two hunting dogs flank the shaft. Below the dogs is a triple disc, or cauldron, and flower symbols. On the back of the slab is a red deer stag and a snake symbol. Many Pictish symbols have yet to be deciphered; they had no written language.

Three miles south-west of Glamis and 10 miles north of Dundee, Eassie is another village whose church is dedicated to Fergus. Beside the ruined church there is a fine cross slab dating from the eighth or ninth century – close to the time of Fergus' death – and it is decorated with interlacing. Above its arms stand two angels; below, a huntsman and his hounds chase a red deer stag. On the other side, Adam is depicted eating the apple of knowledge in the Garden of Eden. Fergus died at Glamis, where his relics were kept for 700 years until an abbot of Scone removed them to his own church to inter them in a more splendid marble tomb. His arm was enshrined in Aberdeen.

## Fillan

The son of a Munster chieftain, Fillan became a monk and went to Scotland in the eighth century with his mother Kentigerna and her brother Comgan, who had been driven out of Leinster by a coalition of neighbouring rulers. The family settled on the Scottish west coast, where there are a number of dedications to Comgan and Kentigerna. Fillan travelled eastwards and spent some time as a hermit in a cave at Pittenweem in Fife.

The small town of Pittenweem is on the north shore of the Firth of Forth, 17 miles east of Glenrothes. The town's name means 'place of the cave'; as we have seen, 'weem' is a transliteration of *uaimh*, the Gaelic word for 'cave'. A cave was warm in

*Dochart Falls, Killin, site of Fillan's mill.*

winter and cool in summer, and if it looked out to sea, it encouraged prayer. The rock plug containing Fillan's cave stands among fishermen's cottages in Cove Wynd, a steep road leading down to the old harbour. The cave was restored in 1935; it is a large one, with two outer chambers, the second of which branches into two more (see *colour plate 7*). An altar has been erected in the cavern to the right, while a freshwater pool in the left-hand one provided Fillan with drinking water. He is said to have left the cave to become abbot of a nearby monastery, where he remained for some years.

According to his legend, recorded in the *Aberdeen Breviary* dating from 1507, Fillan felt called to 'wander for God', so he resigned from his monastery on the Fife coast and travelled westwards into the Highlands. He is said to have retired to Glen Dochart, building a mill at Killin, at the head of Loch Tay, beside the rushing water of the Dochart Falls. Monks who trained in Ireland knew how to construct mills and grind flour; they developed a horizontal mill wheel, which could be used where there was little water, and they brought their technology to the British mainland.

According to tradition, Fillan sat on a stone under an ash tree near the mill at Killin to preach to the local people. The mill often became the focal point of a settlement, since in a small community the miller supervised the sowing of seed and the cutting of peat to fuel the mill's oven, which might also be the village bakery. Fillan's feast day, 9 January, is still a holiday for the mill-workers at Killin. The modern parish church houses a seven-sided Celtic font, carved from a huge boulder. In the grounds of the large hotel next door are the ruins of the medieval church and cemetery dedicated to Fillan. The saint had a reputation for curing the sick. His eight healing stones have always been kept at Fillan's Mill, which now houses the Breadalbane Folklore Centre. These large black and grey stones, smoothed by the river, were considered to heal different parts of the body. A large skull-shaped stone with two 'eye sockets', for example, was invoked for diseases of the head. People still come to hold Fillan's stones and pray for healing.

To the west of Glen Dochart, people bathed in Fillan's Pool, a shallow stretch of the River Dochart at Auchtertyre, as a cure for insanity: deranged people were bathed in the river, wrapped in straw and then taken to Fillan's ruined priory, half a mile to the south-east, on Kirkton Farm. Here they spent the night with their head in the stone font, with Fillan's bell placed above them. Cures were sought as late as the nineteenth century. Fillan was buried nearby; his hand bell survives and his staff, encased in a delicate medieval reliquary, is now in the Royal Museum of Scotland, Edinburgh.

## Finbar

The patron of Cork, Finbar lived in the seventh century; his name means 'white crown' or 'white head'. His father was said to be a smith who married a slave girl. Finbar studied under Bishop MacCuirp at Macroom, and later became a hermit at Gougane Barra. He established his chief monastery in Cork, at the mouth of the River Lee, which rises in Gougane Barra Lake. He attracted followers, and Etargabail on the east bank of the lake became a famous school which drew students from southern Ireland. The town of Cork grew around the monastery which Finbar founded there, and this is where he was buried.

Gougane Barra was the centre of Finbar's cult in earlier times, as it is today. It can be found 6 miles east-north-east of Glengariff, where the R584 takes one through the dramatic Pass of Keimaneigh. For almost a mile there are sheer rock faces on either side of the road; ferns and flowering plants cling to crevices in the cliffs. Close to the head of the pass, a narrow road branches north to Gougane Barra Forest Park and Lough. This is a dark lough surrounded on three sides by high hills. It is the source of the River Lee, which falls in cascades down the rocky hillside and, in times of heavy rain, fills the whole valley with the sound of rushing water.

*Church on Finbar's Island, Gougane Barra.*

Gougane Barra means 'Finbar's rocky cave'; Finbar's monastery was on a small island in the lough. The island is connected to the shore by a causeway, and contains a tiny chapel and the ruins of monastic buildings. Eight small circular cells surround the complex, and a modern church has been erected on the island. An ancient cemetery and Finbar's well can be seen beside the entrance to the causeway leading to the island. There is an annual pilgrimage here on the Sunday nearest to 25 September, Finbar's feast day. Finbar probably remained in southern Ireland, but his followers travelled widely; Barra in the Scottish Hebrides is named after him.

## Finnian of Clonard

The large and famous monastery of Clonard, 34 miles west of Dublin, was founded by Finnian (d. c. 549). His tenth-century *Life*, preserved in the *Book of Lismore*, relates that he was born and educated in County Carlow in south-east Ireland, where he made his first three foundations. Finnian then travelled to south Wales, where he spent time in the great Welsh monasteries. He returned to Ireland and established two more communities before settling at Clonard in County Meath. Finnian's *Life* claims that 3000 monks studied at Clonard. So great was Finnian's reputation that he was nicknamed 'Teacher of the saints of Ireland'. When men left Clonard, they took with them a gospel book, a crosier or a reliquary, as they set out to establish their own communities.

Finnian chose a central location, only 30 miles from the east coast, so that monks could easily reach Clonard from mainland Britain and Europe. The settlement was in fertile farmland beside the River Boyne; cows grazing the site today are a reminder that the rich pasture could support a large community. There have been sample

*Early lavabo, Clonard churchyard.*

excavations at the extensive monastic site, but few remains have been uncovered. Down a signed grassy track, a modern church stands within an ancient graveyard. Set in the ground near the church porch is a large rectangular stone basin or *lavabo* which originally contained water for washing. This may date from early times; it is 2ft 2in by 21in, and is 15in deep. Its brackish water was said to cause death to animals but to cure warts.

Another artefact which has survived is a tiny elaborate bucket, bound with a bronze hoop; its handle clasps are decorated with fine carving and precious stones. The bucket was perhaps used to contain holy water. Finnian's relics were enshrined at Clonard until the monastery was destroyed in 887. It was rebuilt in the twelfth century, and its monks adopted the Augustinian rule. A magnificent fifteenth-century font of grey marble limestone survives from the abbey. It can be seen in the apse behind the high altar in the modern Catholic church beside the busy N6 in Clonard village. Lively scenes are carved on its panels: Joseph leads a donkey by its halter as the Holy Family flees into Egypt and a smiling Bishop Finnian raises his hand in blessing, while an angel beside him holds a gospel book.

Twelve leading Irish monks were known as Finnian's 'Twelve Apostles'. Among them were Ciarán of Clonmacnoise, Kevin of Glendalough, Brendan and Columba. Several of Finnian's 'apostles' had died before his lifetime or had not yet been born, but the list indicates Clonard's considerable influence. Finnian was a correspondent of the British monk, Gildas. The *Penitential of Finnian* was probably written at Clonard. This is a manual of punishments for crimes, based partly on Irish and Welsh sources, and also on the writings of Jerome and Cassian. Much of it, however, is original. It is the oldest of the Irish penitentials, which made an important contribution to the Church's understanding of pastoral care. Like many other Irish monks, Finnian died of the plague.

## Garmon

Garmon was a local saint of Powys in north Wales; a scattering of churches and wells are dedicated to him in Denbigh, Montgomery, Radnor and Flint. The large churchyard of Llanarmon-yn-Iâl (or 'church of Garmon in the hills') may be the site of his monastery. It is set in the Denbighshire uplands, 5 miles south-east of Ruthin; the present church dates from the thirteenth century. The Tudor antiquarian, John Leland, describes an annual pilgrimage to Llanarmon-yn-Iâl, when offerings were made in the presence of a statue of Garmon dressed in priestly vestments. The church was given a double nave to accommodate the large number of pilgrims who came to honour Garmon. A recumbent effigy of a medieval monk named Cyrus can be seen in the church, which also possesses a beautiful brass candelabra dating from 1450, depicting the Virgin and Child (the babe is now missing) enfolded by vine leaves; this may have come from Valle Crucis abbey, whose monks owned the church.

St German's cathedral at Peel on the Isle of Man, halfway along its west coast, is also named after Garmon; it occupies the crest of St Patrick's Isle at Peel. Until the eighteenth century this was a tidal islet, accessible on foot at low tide. There is now a causeway leading to the island, which is dominated by the medieval cathedral of St German and a later castle. The island was inhabited from early times and a number of roundhouses dating from 400 BC have been excavated. These homesteads were very large – up to 10m in diameter – and one included a grain store which later burnt down. Their inhabitants grew cereals and raised cattle; they wore textiles, worked metals and traded with the outside world.

Later, there was a Christian community on St Patrick's Isle. Its first buildings have not survived, but they would have been small cells of wattle and daub, with a church of heavier timber and a few more communal buildings. From the seventh century onwards there was an extensive cemetery at the southern end of the island, near the medieval cathedral. Lintel graves and crosses dating from the seventh and eighth centuries were found beneath the south transept of the cathedral.

The ruins of a church, a chapel and a round tower survive from the Celtic monastery, each dating in part from the tenth century. St Patrick's church was constructed of roughly dressed local red sandstone. It had *antae*, or side walls, projecting beyond the line of the gables; this style of building was common in Ireland. St Patrick's chapel is smaller, but of similar construction. An altar slab was found when the two buildings were restored in 1873. It is decorated with five small crosses set within a larger one, and formed the front panel of a stone altar. Near St Patrick's church is a squat round tower, 15m high. Four windows facing the compass points near the top indicate that this was its original height. It, too, is built of red sandstone; its battlemented parapet was added in about 1600.

The monastery was ravaged by Viking raiders, and the little island became a base for Norse settlers. They built a fort of timber, or pile, which gave Peel its name. Excavations beneath Peel castle have produced evidence of at least seven pagan burials within the Christian cemetery. The richest grave was that of a Viking woman

*Tenth-century chapel with antae, St German's cathedral, Peel.*

who was interred with her cooking spit, a symbol of domestic power in Scandinavia. At her side were her knives and sewing equipment, including a workbox, needle and shears. She wore a magnificent necklace of 73 glass, amber and jet beads, some already centuries old. The burial of a wealthy pagan Norsewoman in a Christian cemetery reflects the mixture of material cultures and beliefs that have shaped the Manx people.

## Guénolé

Guénolé was a sixth-century monk widely venerated in Brittany, where he has some 50 dedications, and in Britain, where another six churches are named after him, including those of Gunwalloe and Landewednack on the Lizard in Cornwall. Abbot Wrdisten's late ninth-century *Life of Winwaloe* describes how he was born of noble British parents who had emigrated to Brittany. He was trained in Budoc's monastery, after which he founded a community on the Isle of Tibidy and another at Landévennec, in Finistère, where he died.

Guénolé's name is spelt in various ways: St Winwaloe's church at Gunwalloe in Cornwall is named after him. Set in Church Cove, above a sandy beach, this little church is on the west coast of the Lizard, 3 miles south of Helston; its freestanding tower is built into the cliff. A wooden panel survives from the fifteenth-century rood screen, with painted figures of the apostles. Winwaloe's well could formerly be found between the church and the beach, but the sea has now engulfed it. It was still in use in the nineteenth century, but it filled with sand and pebbles at each high tide. The antiquarian, Quiller Couch, describes how one day each year was set aside for cleaning out the well; it was called Gunwalloe day, and was celebrated 'with much merriment'.

The most southerly parish in Britain, Landewednack, on the Lizard peninsula, is also dedicated to Guénolé; it may be a

*St Winnow church: bench end depicting a Tudor ship blown by the wind.*

daughter house of his Breton monastery at Landévennec. The church has a fine twelfth-century Norman doorway decorated with zigzag patterns and a medieval squint or hole cut in the wall to enable worshippers in the south transept to see the high altar. The church also contains an elaborately carved wooden prayer desk constructed from the rood screen of Ruan Major church, now derelict, which is in the same parish.

Winnow (or Winnoc) is another variant of the name Guénolé. Beautifully situated beside the estuary of the River Fowey, St Winnow church is built on the site of a chapel of St Winnow. It is on a minor road between Lerryn and Lostwithiel; there are freshwater springs under and around the large medieval church. It contains an unusual fifteenth-century granite font: four angels hold hands round its bowl and a Latin inscription encircles its rim, which can be translated as: 'See, the beloved of the true God shall be baptised with the Holy Spirit.' The church contains some magnificent carved bench ends: one depicts a man wearing a Cornish kilt and drinking cider from a leather bottle. He wears a bonnet and a long-sleeved tunic with a pleated skirt and leather shoes, a style of clothing worn around 1530. Another bench end depicts a Tudor ship of about 1485 blown by the wind; a ship was launched at St Winnow as late as 1701.

## Gunwalloe: see Guénolé

## Gwbert: see Cubert

## Gwynhoedl

Gwynhoedl, or Vendesetl, may have been a Romano-British monk from south Wales who travelled north as a missionary. Llangwynnadl is 10 miles west of Pwllheli, on the north coast of the Lleyn peninsula. It became one of the main stopping places on the Saints' Way to Bardsey, since it was only 5 miles to Aberdaron, the crossing point for Bardsey Island. A medieval monk's hand bell survives from the church: it is of cast bronze and is 17cm high; its handle has animal-headed terminals. It is now in the National Museum of Wales, Cardiff.

Gwynhoedl's tombstone is at Llanbedrog, 4 miles south-west of Pwllheli, on the south coast of the Lleyn peninsula. However, the people of Llangwynnadl were keen to claim that their saint was buried among them, and a Latin inscription carved round a pillar in the nave around 1520 reads: *S. Gwynhoedl iacet hic* ('Saint Gwynhoedl lies here'). At the same time, a second and third nave were added to the church to accommodate the

*Replica of Gwynhoedl's bell, in Llangwynnadl church.*

crowds of pilgrims. A fine new font was also carved, featuring the heads of King Henry VIII and Bishop Skeffington of Bangor. Across the small river that flows past the church to the sea, a large field was named *Cae Eisteddfa*, or Hospice Field. Here pilgrims could camp before continuing their journey to or from Bardsey Island.

## Helen (Elen Luyddoc)

It was formerly believed that a Celtic princess named Helen was the wife of Magnus Maximus, the self-styled emperor of Britain, Gaul and Spain from 383 to 388. Scholars now consider the story of Helen to be unlikely, although Maximus and Elen are named in early Welsh genealogies. According to late medieval legend, Helen accompanied her husband to Europe. She was said to have returned to Britain after her husband's defeat and death, with her sons, Publicus and Constantine (or Peblig and Cystennin in Welsh). Churches are dedicated to each of them in north and south Wales.

Helen was thought to be responsible for a network of ancient trackways near the Welsh coast called *Sarn Helen* and in places they can still be seen. In *The Dream of Maxen Wledig*, a story chanted by medieval Welsh bards, Helen orders the roads to be constructed to improve travel between fortresses for the royal entourage:

> One day the emperor [Magnus Maximus] went to hunt at Carmarthen … and he built a castle there, with very many soldiers. Then Helen decided to have roads built between the castles throughout Britain. That is why they are called Helen Luyddoc's roads, because she was British-born, and Britons made these great roads only for her. (*The Mabinogion*, 1997, p. 56)

Llanbeblig, close to the Roman fort of Segontium, on the eastern edge of Caernarfon in north Wales, is the only church dedicated to Peblig, who was held to be Helen's son. *The Dream of Maxen Wledig* gives an early account of Caernarfon, filtered through medieval eyes. Segontium was built in AD 77 and remained the military

*Peblig's church at Llanbeblig, near Caernarfon.*

and administrative centre of north-west Wales until 394. Up to a thousand soldiers were stationed here. A Roman altar can be seen in Llanbeblig churchyard, which is on the A4085 Portmadoc Road on the same side as the Roman fort, a little lower down the hill.

## Ia

One of Cornwall's female saints, Ia is the patroness of St Ives on the north Cornish coast. The earliest traditions about Ia are found in the *Life of Gwinear*, written by the Breton cleric Anselm in about 1300. Here we read that Hya, a high-born Irish nun, arrived too late at the Irish coast to accompany Gwinear and his companions to Cornwall, but a leaf enlarged itself to the size of a boat and carried her there; from a cliff top, a curragh can resemble a curled leaf. Ia's tomb was in St Ives church, and her holy well is in a stone building outside the lower wall of the cemetery. Other Cornish chapels and wells are named after her. In the region of Finistère in western Brittany is the settlement of Plouyé (meaning 'place of Ia'). This is a large and possibly early parish, suggesting that her cult may have originated in Brittany. Just outside the east wall of Plouyé church is a tall, fluted Gallo-Roman memorial pillar, confirming that this was an early holy site.

*Ia's holy well, St Ives, Cornwall.*

# Illtud

The seventh-century *Life of Samson* tells us that Illtud (c. 425–505) was a Breton soldier of fortune who came to Wales to fight under a Glamorgan chieftain. Dissatisfied with a soldier's life, he became a monk and his wife became a nun. Illtud was ordained a priest by Germanus, bishop of Auxerre, in about 445, and five years later he established a monastery at Llanilltud Fawr, meaning 'Illtud's great church' (in English, Llantwit Major) on the south coast of Wales, in the Vale of Glamorgan, 9 miles west of Barry. Illtud may have lived here as a hermit before he attracted followers and built a church with a school and a monastery. Dubricius prepared Illtud as a monk and marked out the monastic enclosure. The author of Samson's *Life* describes how young Samson was taken by his parents to Illtud's famous school. He explains that Illtud combined Christian, classical and Druidic learning: he was the most learned of all Britons in scripture and philosophy, poetry and rhetoric, grammar and arithmetic. He was of Druid descent, most wise and able to foretell the future. The writer adds a personal comment: 'I have been in his magnificent monastery.'

This became the most famous Celtic monastery in Wales. It is hidden in a small river valley, where it would have been out of sight of pirates; nearby St Donats provided a natural harbour. Inside the church there is a fine collection of monuments from the monastery. One of the earliest of these, the St Illtud (or 'Samson') Cross, may date from soon after Illtud's death. Its shaft, which was probably once capped by a wheel cross, contains two Latin inscriptions. The east face reads: 'Samson placed this cross for his soul', and the west face reads: '(For the souls of) Illtud, Samson the King, Samuel, Ebisar'.

There is also a pillar inscribed to an abbot named Samson, and a cross with a disc head inscribed in Latin half-uncial script: 'In the name of God the Father and the Holy Spirit. Houelt prepared this cross for the soul of Res, his father.' Houelt was probably Hywel ap Rhys, a ninth-century King of Glywysing, the land between the River Tawe and the River Usk. The monastery was so important that kings were brought here for burial. Hywel was a subject of King Alfred of Wessex in 884. The shallow triangular key patterns of the Houelt cross, arranged in two paved bands, recall motifs found in illuminated manuscripts. Both its inscription and the style of decoration resemble examples of the same date in Ireland.

Today there are two medieval churches at Llanilltud Fawr, built end to end. The Celtic church probably stood on the site of the present

*Sandstone cross slab, late ninth or early tenth century, Llanilltud Fawr.*

west church, in which the crosses now stand. This was rebuilt by the Normans in about 1100. The archway over the south door dates from this time. The Norman font also survives; its bowl is decorated with fish-scale patterns. In the thirteenth century the east church was built for the canons of the medieval monastery, while the parishioners probably continued to worship in the west church. Behind the modern rood that decorates the chancel arch of the canons' church are the remains of fourteenth-century wall paintings. There is a fine fifteenth-century reredos of carved stone behind the high altar of the east church.

In the fifteenth century the west church was rebuilt and its arched roof of oak dates from this time. In time, however, the west church fell into ruin. John Wesley preached here in 1777 and recorded in his diary:

> About eleven, I read prayers and preached in Llantwit Major church to a very numerous congregation. I have not seen either so large or so handsome a church since I left England. It was sixty yards long, but one end of it is now in ruins. I suppose it has been abundantly the most beautiful as well as the most spacious church in Wales.

Illtud's monastery was one of the most influential of its time. Famous monks and scholars studied there, including Samson, Gildas and Paul Aurelian. Illtud is said to have drained land for cultivation and to have introduced an improved form of plough. He sailed back to Brittany with some shiploads of corn to relieve a famine. There are seven dedications to Illtud in south-east Wales. There is one in the north, on the coast 2 miles north-west of Dolgellau. It is named Llanelltyd, using the northern, Brittonic, spelling of his name, instead of the usual southern, Gaelic form.

# Indract

Possibly a mid ninth-century abbot of Iona or Kells, Indract is described in the Irish *Martyrology of Tallaght* (c. 800) as 'a martyr for the faith at Glastonbury'. According to his early twelfth-century *Life*, Indract was the son of an Irish prince. When he was a deacon he visited Rome with 12 companions. On the way home they stopped at Glastonbury, bringing with them sacks of celery seed, presumably to plant in their Irish monastery, and they stayed for the night near Shapwick. King Ine of Wessex (688–726) was at South Petherton with his entourage, and one of his thegns murdered Indract and his companions, thinking their sacks contained gold. Indract was buried at Shapwick, the mother church of the area. The martyr's relics were taken by King Ine to Glastonbury abbey, where they were buried beside the high altar of the old church, which was destroyed by fire in 1184. The author of Indract's *Life* says he has taken the story from an old English source.

A Roman road ran from the Fosse Way past Shapwick to the sea. There was a Romano-British villa at Shapwick, and in 1988 Britain's largest hoard of early Roman coins was found here. It was buried around AD 230, and was the equivalent of about 10 years' pay for a legionary soldier. Had the Saxon thegns been better informed, they might not have gone to the trouble of murdering Indract!

*Excavations at Old Church Farm, Shapwick, 2000.*

The original site of the village is at Old Church Farm, half a mile out of Shapwick, east of the present church. Excavation here has provided evidence of a Roman settlement and of a large medieval building lower down the field from the site of the former church. The photograph shows the building being excavated by Time Team under the direction of Mick Aston in 2000; in the foreground is a Roman boundary ditch. Near the church there was evidence of a Bronze Age hut, and a large spring emerged on the east side of the church. This site had experienced continuous settlement over a long period. In medieval times the villagers moved to a new location half a mile west of their original settlement; this is where the present fourteenth-century church can be found. St Indract's holy well is near the site of the old church, on the corner of the road leading into Shapwick. Another holy well is dedicated to Indract in St Dominick parish in Cornwall, near Halton Quay, high above the River Tamar.

## Juliot

Juliot was a female saint with three dedications on the north Cornish coast; the name Juliot is a diminutive form of Juliana. The twelfth-century *Life of Nectan* from Hartland abbey lists Juliana as one of the 12 daughters of Brychan, and the church on the rocky fortress of Tintagel may be dedicated to her. She is also conflated with Julitta, who was supposedly martyred in Tarsus in Asia Minor around 304, together with her son Cyricus. The mother and child have three dedications in Cornwall: the child martyr Cyricus was a patron of children, and there are further sites honouring the mother and child in Devon and Somerset.

*Juliot's ruined chapel, Tintagel.*

In the sixth century, the rocky headland of Tintagel (see *colour plate 18*) was a chieftain's stronghold. Situated 3 miles south-west of Boscastle, it is almost an island; its Celtic name probably means 'narrow-necked fortress'. It is likely that Celtic chieftains moved frequently, for their entourage required more food than any district could supply for long. Tintagel may therefore have been occupied for only a few months each year. However, its rulers lived in style, and more imported pottery has been found here than at any other sixth-century British or Irish site: pieces of huge oil containers from Tunisia, smaller handled jars from Byzantium and fine red dishes from Carthage. In 1998 fragments of a sixth-century Spanish glass flagon were also found. Some of the red dishes at Tintagel are stamped with a cross.

Near the top of the fortress are the remains of Juliot's chapel. It was built in about 1000, and the east end was added around 1230, when a medieval castle was built on the site. The chapel's Norman font can be seen in the parish church of St Materiana, on the mainland below the fort. This church is set within what was perhaps the royal burial ground for the chieftains who lived in the stronghold above. A fourth-century Roman milestone preserved in the church was brought here from the Roman campsite on the cliff.

From the sixth century until the twelfth, the fortress of Tintagel was abandoned; Juliot's chapel, however, remained in use. Unexpectedly, there are three wells on the rocky outcrop as a supply of fresh water was vital for a fort. Juliot's twin wells are just beyond her chapel; since they are fenced in, they can be easily spotted. There is a magnificent view from the chapel along the coast in both directions.

# Justinian

Justinian was a sixth-century hermit who lived on Ramsey Island opposite St David's in Pembrokeshire; he was said to be a friend of David. According to his twelfth-century *Life*, he was a Breton of noble birth who became a priest and left his country as a pilgrim for Christ; he was later killed by his servants. A holy well is named after him on the mainland opposite Ramsey Island; beside it is a ruined chapel restored by Bishop Vaughan in the early sixteenth century.

There is an early church dedicated to Justinian at Llanstinan in the valley of the River Cleddau, 10 miles north-east of St David's. It is built inside an ancient stone circle. Seven springs are said to rise on the site, which was once beside a lake. The village of Scleddau, which surrounded the church, has now disappeared, although rambler roses from cottage gardens still grow in the hedgerows. The medieval church was once the centre of the village; there are remains of the old school within the enclosure.

The church is built on Celtic foundations and has a 'squinch', or small triangular room, between the nave and the chancel, on the site where a hermit's cell adjoined the church. By living in a hut built against the church wall, a medieval hermit could retain his privacy, yet also be present at church services. A squinch is a feature of a number of early Pembrokeshire churches. Llanstinan is 2 miles south-east of Fishguard, near the A40. After leaving Fishguard, watch for a sign to Llanstinan on the left, beside a disused quarry. Park in the layby, then walk for 10 minutes along the signed footpath, through the Cleddau valley. Turn left through a farmyard; the church is on low ground in front of you.

*Llanstinan church: small triangular room (left) for a hermit.*

# Kea

St Kea was an obscure saint who, according to his *Life*, was born in Wales and migrated to Brittany. It is possible that an early monastery dedicated to St Kea lies beneath the parish church of Leigh, on the northern edge of the ancient town of Street, 2 miles south-west of Glastonbury in Somerset. The parish church, now dedicated to the Holy Trinity, was anciently claimed as one of Glastonbury's seven churches. Between the thirteenth and the sixteenth centuries it was dedicated to St Gildas. Also associated with the district, and from an earlier date, is the place name *Lantokay*, which appears in a grant of land by Bishop Haeddi of Winchester to the abbot of Glastonbury in 677–92.

The name *Lantokay* (or 'church site of Kea') is very early. In fact, this is the earliest recorded British *lan* site, predating those in Cornish and Welsh records by 200 years. The churchyard is a large oval enclosure, which suggests that this is likely to have been a Celtic monastery. There was space for a cemetery surrounding the church, and dwellings for monks, craftsmen and labourers with their families. An earthwork inside its curved western boundary would have been the monastery's surrounding wall. The site had already been occupied: Roman potsherds, including Samian ware, and an Iron Age coin were found in the graveyard. An estate of three hides associated with the church was probably land tended by the monks. In 1503, the first enclosure beyond St Kea's church was known as *Ankerhey*, or 'anchorite's enclosure'. To the west of the church, old maps name a former manor house *Brutessayshe* (British ash); the ash was a holy tree in Celtic times. It is possible, therefore, that the first monks chose this site because it was already considered holy by the local people. Three ash trees were recorded as growing here in 1503.

*The church of Saints Gildas and Kea, Street.*

There is evidence of Kea's cult in Brittany, where his *Life* was written; Landkey in Devon and Old Kea in Cornwall (possibly the site of another early monastery) may also be named after him. At Landkey, the high banks of the churchyard outline the Celtic enclosure; its settlement was called *Landechei* in 1166, a name resembling that of Street's church. The Romano-British name of this saint derives from the Latin *Caius*, and he gave his name to Sir Kay, one of King Arthur's knights. Kea's feast day was celebrated on 5 November, and he was invoked for toothache.

## Kenneth

The sixth-century Irish abbot Kenneth, or Cainnech, was born in Derry, the son of a bard. Adomnán mentions him several times in his *Life of Columba*. He founded a number of communities, including Drumahose in Derry; his chief monastery was at Aghaboe in County Laois. From time to time he visited Columba on Iona, where a church and a cemetery are named after him. A number of churches honour him in Scotland, chief of them being Inchkenneth on Mull. Others include Kilchennich on the island of Tiree, Kilchainie on South Uist and Cambuskenneth on the mainland, near Stirling.

Kenneth was a close friend of Columba, and Adomnán recounts how he arrived safely on Iona during a storm, through Columba's prayers:

> One day when there was a violent storm and waves of daunting height, [Columba] was sitting indoors and giving instructions to the brothers. 'Prepare the guest-house quickly,' he said, 'and draw water to wash the visitors' feet.' One of the brothers then said, 'Who can cross the Sound in safety, narrow though it is, on so stormy and perilous a day as this?' At this the saint declared, 'In spite of the storm the Almighty has granted a calm to a holy and elect man who will arrive among us before evening.' And, behold, after a while that same day the ship carrying Saint Cainnech for which the brothers had waited arrived ...

St Kenneth's cathedral is in Aghaboe, 10 miles east-south-east of Roscrea. We hear of one of its later abbots, Virgilius, who in 739

*Aghaboe cathedral: arched alcove in the south chapel.*

resigned from his position in order to become a missionary. He travelled to Austria, and was bishop of Salzburg from 749 to 784. In 913 the abbey at Aghaboe was plundered by Norsemen. In 1052 a great church was built and Kenneth's relics were enshrined in it. In 1116 the monastic city was severely damaged by fire; a new church was built in 1189.

From 1111 to 1200, Aghaboe abbey was the cathedral church of Ossory diocese, but the building continued to have a chequered history: in 1346, St Kenneth's church and shrine were destroyed by fire during a Norman attack. The present large-scale building was constructed in 1132 and given to the Dominican Order. It was suppressed in 1540, but Dominican friars continued to serve here secretly until the eighteenth century. The building is now a ruin, though a few interesting features adorn its otherwise plain walls: there is a delicately carved alcove in the south chapel with a fourteenth-century ogee arch.

# Kentigern

A Briton who became bishop of Glasgow in the sixth century, Kentigern's name means 'Chief Prince'. We know little about him, but we do know that he existed, since his name appears in early texts. In the twelfth century a Cumbrian monk named Jocelyn, from Furness abbey, wrote his *Life*, although it is largely based on legend. He relates that Kentigern was the illegitimate son of a British princess. Her angry father set her adrift in a coracle and she floated across the Firth of Forth, landing on a beach at Culross, on the Fife coast. Here, she lit a fire and gave birth to her son. There was an early monastery at Culross, where Kentigern is said to have trained as a monk.

It appears that when an anti-Christian chieftain came to power, Kentigern fled south, first to Cumbria and then to Wales. Jocelyn describes Kentigern arriving at Carlisle and proceeding to Crosthwaite. A number of other churches in Cumbria are dedicated to Kentigern, some using his pet name, Mungo (meaning 'My Dear One'). Jocelyn recounts how Kentigern arrived in Wales and eventually gained permission from

*The monastery's well in the crypt, Glasgow cathedral.*

Maelgwyn Gwynedd to build a monastery at a site now named St Asaph. A wild white boar showed Kentigern where he should build his church, a feature in the stories of other Celtic saints, such as Ciarán of Saighir and Cyngar. Kentigern's ablest student was said to have been Asaph; according to Jocelyn, when the political scene shifted in Strathclyde, Kentigern left Asaph in charge of his Welsh community and returned to Glasgow with a large group of monks.

Jocelyn relates that Kentigern spent the last years of his long life among his brothers. He records a tradition that Kentigern's death occurred on 13 January, at the end of the octave, or week, of celebration following the feast of the Epiphany. He died comfortably in a warm bath, symbolic for Jocelyn's readers of the bath of baptism. The story demonstrated that Kentigern was reborn into heavenly life. In the Eastern Churches, candidates were immersed for baptism on the feast of the Epiphany. The festival recalled how the wise men followed a star to Bethlehem and how angels appeared to guide them. Jocelyn weaves these strands into his story.

Kentigern's tomb is in the crypt of Glasgow cathedral. Arcading from the plinth of his thirteenth-century shrine can still be seen. Built into the wall of the lower church, or crypt, is the well which provided his monks with water for both drinking and bathing. The first stone-built cathedral was dedicated in 1136 in the presence of King David I; the present building dates from the thirteenth century.

## Kessóg

One of the early Irish monks who settled in Strathclyde, Kessóg (d. c. 520) was born at Cashel in southern Ireland, of the royal family of Munster. He travelled to Scotland where he became a monk and, later, bishop of the ancient earldom of Lennox. Kessóg built a monastery on a small island in Loch Lomond named Inchtavannach or 'Isle of the Monks'. Older people still call it 'Isle of the Two Bells' in Gaelic, referring to the bells with which the monks summoned one another to prayer in the chapel. The wooded island is a mile long; it was an ideal location for a monastery, being sufficiently isolated to afford an opportunity for prayer, but close enough to the lakeshore to provide easy access to centres of population.

The nearest town is Luss on the mainland a mile to the north-west, beside the mouth of Luss Water, at the point where it flows into Loch Lomond. Its church was the site of Kessóg's shrine in medieval times. He was known as a zealous preacher and was said to heal the sick with a herb named *lus* in Gaelic (similar to *fleur de lys* in French), which may be the yellow flag that grows near the mouth of Luss Water. In Luss churchyard, two sixth-century grave markers, each carved with a Latin cross, and a seventh-century four-holed cross indicate the continued presence of Christians at Luss. An impressive Viking hogback tomb can also be seen in the churchyard, embellished with neat rows of imitation roof tiles. It is designed to represent a house of the dead; around its sides, arcading rises from a row of columns.

The grave slab dates from the Norse invasion led by King Hakon of Norway, and is a reminder of one of his most daring raids. In 1263 Hakon's long ships sailed into the Firth of Clyde and continued northwards through Loch Long. The boats were

*Kessóg's Mound, Callander.*

then hauled overland to Loch Lomond, across the tarbert (or narrow strip of land at the head of an isthmus), a useful shortcut between two stretches of water. The village of Tarbet derives its name from this fact. Loch Lomond lies only 1½ miles to the east of Loch Long, and from their new vantage point the Norsemen proceeded to ravage Luss and much of the surrounding countryside. King Hakon then travelled 20 miles round the coast to fight the Battle of Largs. The hogback tomb at Luss may commemorate one of his warriors.

There is another dedication to Kessóg in Callander, at the foot of the Trossach Hills, 14 miles north-west of Stirling. The River Teith winds to the south of the Trossachs, and the town of Callander grew beside a shallow crossing point. A church dedicated to Kessóg once stood here; its walled graveyard can be seen close to the river, beside the road leading into the town. Between the churchyard and a large car park is *Tom na Chessaig* or Kessóg's Mound, a grassy hillock where the monk is said to have gathered the people and preached to them. The mound is best approached by entering Callander from the south, on the A81. The ancient cemetery is just over the bridge, and the mound is beyond it, further to the left.

Kessóg was said to have been murdered at Bandry, within sight of his island monastery, a mile south of Luss. Local Christians built a cairn of stones over the place where he fell. It was destroyed when the shore road was constructed in 1761. A carved stone head, perhaps representing Kessóg, was found beneath it; the small sculpture now rests on a window ledge in the church at Luss, which continued to be the centre of Kessóg's cult. In 1315, King Robert Bruce declared the church and its surrounding area a place of sanctuary, an offering 'to God and the blessed St Kessóg for ever of three miles round the church as by land and water'. Here criminals could take refuge from the law, and presumably go into hiding on the islands and in the glens. Kessóg's shrine was visited well after the Reformation. The remains of a medieval chapel can be seen in Luss churchyard. There are two sixteenth-century references to Kessóg's hand bell, and the Colquhoun family are hereditary keepers of his *bachuil*, or monk's staff.

# Kevin

Kevin was born in the early sixth century of a noble Leinster family ousted from kingship. His name, *Cóemhghein*, means 'Fairborn'. The surviving *Lives* of Kevin (d. c. 618) are late and unreliable; the earliest appears to have been written by a monk at Glendalough in the tenth or eleventh century. Kevin was said to have been trained by three wise old monks. While searching for a deserted place in which to live and pray, he came to Glendalough, where he lived in the hollow of a tree, beside the Upper Lake. Later he was ordained as a priest by a bishop named Lugidus, who sent him out with some monks to found a new church in an unidentified place. Here he spent a while 'gathering servants for Christ' before moving with them to Glendalough, where he founded a monastery

Glendalough is famous for its scenic beauty as well as its monastic remains, which are built beside a pass through the Wicklow Mountains and border two lakes: the name *Gleann-dá-loch* means 'Glen of the two lakes'. According to his Latin *Life*, Kevin founded a great monastery in the lower part of the valley where two rivers meet. Once it was established, he entrusted it to the care of responsible monks and returned to the upper valley, a mile to the west, to live once more as a hermit. Here he built a small dwelling in a narrow place between the mountain and the lake, where there were dense woods and clear streams. This area is known as Kevin's Desert. He was said to have fed on sorrel and nettles. Beside the shore, sorrel of unusually fine quality still grows; nettle broth was considered a valuable food at this time and sorrel soup is still much prized.

On a promontory overlooking the Upper Lake, the remains of a circular hut known as Kevin's Cell have been excavated, and there are possible sites of other huts further up the hillside. There is an early church, *Teampall na Skellig*, on a shelf above the Upper Lake, close to 'St Kevin's Bed', a cave in the rock face which may have been a Bronze Age mineshaft. According to tradition, Kevin used this as a shelter. The River Poulanass cascades down the hillside into the Upper Lake on its southern shore, and nearby is the Reefert church, in a grove of hazel trees. This appears to have been a church used by the solitary monks who chose to live in Kevin's Desert.

The Reefert church is a fine eleventh-century building with an early example of a chancel arch. A large stone with four interlinked crosses may have been an altar front; it is now in St Kevin's church in the monastic city. Reefert graveyard is one of the few in which Celtic grave markers are still in their original position, lying flat on the graves, with other slabs and small crosses serving as upright headstones. The name Reefert appears to derive from *Ríg Fearta*, or 'burial place of kings'. The title may date from the late twelfth century when the royal family of the O'Tooles was driven from Kildare into the Wicklow Mountains by the Normans.

*Celtic gravestones, Reefert church, Glendalough.*

After some years as a hermit beside the Upper Lake, Kevin apparently returned to the monastic city to die. His *Life* relates that he sent a party of monks to the hermitage to pray for him. It describes his burial place, 'to the east of the Lower Lake'. This appears to indicate St Mary's church, at the western end of the monastic city. St Mary's is one of the earliest churches on the site; in the eighteenth century it was still venerated as the place of Kevin's burial. Its chancel was probably built in the tenth century, but its nave is considerably earlier.

It is a common opinion that the monks moved to the lower site only after Kevin's death, but it is equally possible that Kevin himself selected this location. The remains of the monastic city here are extensive, with five churches and a round tower. Another two churches were later built further down the valley. The main entrance to the monastery is close to the road, where it crosses the River Glendasan. The present bridge may stand on the site of an earlier one, which the monastery's annals describe as being swept away in the great flood of 1177.

The enclosure is approached by a gateway, the only surviving monastic entrance in Ireland. The impressive building dates from some time after 900. Two fine granite arches survive; its *antae*, or projecting walls, at each end suggest that there was a timber roof. The outline of a large, simple cross is carved on a giant slab beyond the inner arch. This marked out the monastery as a place of sanctuary, where criminals could take refuge from the law. Beyond the arches are preserved the large paving slabs of the original causeway into the monastic city.

St Kevin's church is the best preserved building within the enclosure. Its steeply pitched stone roof is built on the corbel principle, like the beehive huts of Kerry: each stone slopes slightly outwards to throw off the rain. There is a first floor with a loft above, where the monks may have slept. There are holes for beams which supported the first floor, 3.8m above ground level. A small round tower is built into the west gable; a similar belfry was constructed at Trinity church, further down the valley, but it collapsed during a storm in 1818.

*1 Medieval watching chamber (left) and Alban's shrine (right), St Albans cathedral.*

*2 Model of a fourth-century church, Silchester, near Reading.*

3  Octagonal baptismal pool, Chedworth Roman villa.

4  The baptistery wall is uncovered in the Roman villa, Bradford-on-Avon. To the right is the apse mosaic.

5  Statue thought to depict St Antony of Egypt, Padstow church, Cornwall.

6 *Caves at East Wemyss, Fife.*

7  St Fillan's cave, Pittenweem, Fife.

8  Cave at Caiplie, Fife.

9 *Cave at Caiplie, exterior.*

*10 High cross and Romanesque church, Kilmalkedar.*

11  Model of the Saxon monastery of Jarrow, beside the River Don, Tyne and Wear.

12  Model of pebble-board plough, Whithorn.

13  *White pony, Iona.*

14 Creels on the strand, Traighmòr, Iona.

15 St Govan's chapel, St Govan's Head, Pembrokeshire.

16 St Michael's chapel, Roche Rocks, Cornwall.

17  Glastonbury Tor, viewed from Wearyall Hill, Somerset.

18  Tintagel fortress, Cornwall.

19  Early preaching station: St Patrick's Chair, Marown, Isle of Man.

20  Gallarus Oratory, Dingle peninsula, Kerry.

21  West door, Gallarus Oratory, Dingle Peninsula, Ireland.

22 Reconstruction of a monastic altar, Clonmacnoise, Ireland.

23 St Bega's church, Bassenthwaite, at the foot of Mount Skiddaw, Cumbria.

24 *St Patrick's well, Patterdale, Cumbria.*

North of St Kevin's church is a building known as the Priests' House, since priests were buried here in the eighteenth and nineteenth centuries. At the centre of the monastic city is the cathedral, a large building constructed over several hundred years from the ninth century onwards. It is referred to in the annals as 'the abbey' and was an imposing building. Its nave is wider than that of any other Irish church. Outside it stands a tall ringed cross of granite.

The round tower dominates the monastic city. Although it is built at the bottom of the valley, it can be seen by travellers approaching from every direction. It is about 30m high, and a watchman at the top could spot attackers advancing from either end of the valley or over the mountains. At the top, four windows face the compass points; below were six floors, four of them lit by a tiny window. Since a monastery served as a sanctuary not only for people but also for goods and cattle, looting was frequent. Glendalough is recorded as first being burned in 770 and, over the next 400 years, annals note its destruction on 19 occasions. Danes attacked nine times, Irish plunderers once and three times there were accidental fires. During the twelfth-century reforms of the Irish Church, Glendalough was handed over to a group of Augustinian canons, but it was destroyed several times and finally suppressed in the sixteenth century.

His Latin *Life* describes Kevin travelling west across Ireland to visit young Ciarán of Clonmacnoise as he lay stricken with the plague, but Ciarán died before Kevin's arrival. After his death in old age, Kevin was succeeded as abbot by his nephew Molibba, who appears to have been the first bishop of Glendalough.

# Kew

Kewstoke on the Somerset coast, a mile north-east of Weston-super-Mare, may be named after this female saint. Since she is relatively obscure, it is unlikely that Kew's cult owes its origin to later medieval interest in famous Celtic saints of the past. At Kewstoke, the church and graveyard form part of a roughly oval enclosure, which appears to pre-date the surrounding landscape; this suggests the presence of a small religious community here in Celtic times. In *Domesday Book* (1186), Kewstoke appears as *Chiwestoch*. The suffix *stoc* is an Old English place name element which can mean 'a religious place'. It sometimes appears as 'stow' or 'stoke', to replace the lost British name of an early church site.

The small parish church at Kewstoke is now dedicated to St Paul; no record survives of an earlier dedication to St Kew. The late medieval church may reflect an Anglo-Saxon design in its dimensions, height and floor plan. Saxon openings may have been enlarged to become what are rather unusual clerestory windows. A remarkable flight of steps leads from the churchyard up the steep cliff of Worlebury Hill. It is now known as Monk's Steps, but on earlier maps the flight is named St Kew's Steps. A century ago, they rose dramatically between the bare rock face on either side of a gully, but the hillside is now gently wooded.

On a platform halfway up St Kew's Steps are the remains of a stone building 6m by 4m in size, enclosing a pit which was probably a well. This appears to have been

*St Kew's Steps, Kewstoke.*

an early well chapel or baptistery. When it was excavated in the late nineteenth century, finds suggested ritual use in the Iron Age; it continued to be frequented until the late medieval period. A rare piece of early British metalwork, a penannular silver brooch, was found in 1853 at the top of the steps.

There are two other dedications to St Kew: Llangiwa in Monmouthshire and St Kew near Padstow in Cornwall, where she is connected with Docco. A charter of Edgar dating from AD 961 refers to the monastery of St Dochou and St Cywa. By the early eighteenth century the parish believed Kew and Docco to be brother and sister, but there is no early evidence for this.

# Keyne

Described as one of the daughters of Brychan in twelfth-century Welsh genealogies, Keyne has a number of dedications in Wales. A *Life of Keyne* was included in John of Tynmouth's fourteenth-century *Nova Legenda Anglie*. He probably took his information from a longer Welsh *Life of Keyne*, written after the late eleventh century. According to John of Tynmouth, Keyne refused marriage and became a nun. She left Wales and crossed the River Severn in search of solitude. She lived for a while at a place infested with serpents, which she turned into stone. The author is perhaps referring to Keynsham, 4 miles south-east of Bristol, a settlement at a crossing point of the River Avon. Ammonites, which are fossils shaped like coiled serpents, were found here, and may have given rise to the legend. A similar miracle is attributed to Hilda of Whitby, where ammonites also abound.

St Keyne is a village named after this legendary saint near the south Cornish coast, 2 miles south of Liskeard. Keyne's medieval church stands on high ground above the village. Her holy well is in a valley a mile south-east of the church, down a narrow road; it is clearly signed from the road beside the church. The stone well house was restored in 1932. Above the well there used to be four holy trees, which were described by various antiquarians. In 1602, Richard Carew wrote:

*Keyne's holy well at St Keyne.*

> Four trees of divers kinde,
> Withy, Oke, Elme and Ash,
> Make with their roots an archèd roofe,
> Whose floore this spring doth wash.

The trees died and were replaced in the early eighteenth century. These trees have also gone. The church of St Martin-by-Looe was formerly dedicated to Keyne, and Kenwyn, on the northwestern edge of Truro, may also be named after her.

## Lleuddad

Close to the tip of the Lleyn peninsula, Aberdaron was traditionally important as the place of departure for pilgrims to Bardsey Island. The church is dedicated to two of Cadfan's followers, Hywyn and Lleuddad. Hywyn was said to have been Cadfan's steward, and chaplain to the monks on Bardsey. According to sources of late date, Lleuddad succeeded Cadfan as abbot of Bardsey. A field on the island is known as 'Lleuddad's Garden'; on the mainland, a cave at Aberdaron is named after him, as is a well in Bryncroes parish, 4 miles east of Aberdaron. Its water was renowned for curing sick people and animals.

The lower course of the church at Aberdaron has been buried by drifting sand. It has a Norman porch, and by the twelfth century it had a sanctuary seat – a stone chair in which those taking refuge from the law could claim immunity before sailing to safety in another land. This was a *clas* church: a monastery without a rule, whose headship was hereditary. The Normans destroyed the *clas* system since they preferred to control churches in their territory, but because of its remoteness Aberdaron

*Lleuddad's well, Bryncroes.*

remained a *clas* church until the Reformation. In the fifteenth century the church was doubled in size to accommodate pilgrims.

Great numbers of people made the difficult crossing to Bardsey Island throughout medieval times. They travelled along the Lleyn peninsula, and spent the final night before their sea crossing at Aberdaron. A hospice where they slept is known as 'The Great Kitchen' (*Y Gegin Fawr*); the present building dates from about 1300. Here travellers could rest in comfort before their rough journey by sea. There were two embarkation points near Aberdaron; one of these was at Brach-y-Pwyll, where the foundations of a chapel are visible in the turf above the shore. Down among the rocks is *Ffynnon Fair* ('St Mary's well'), a freshwater spring visible at low tide, but it is difficult to find. Here travellers could fill their water bottles before they embarked.

# Llôlan

Llôlan is said to have been one of the many Welsh monks who fled from Powys after the Battle of Chester. In the course of the battle, which took place around 613, Ethelfrid, the pagan King of the Angles, massacred many Christians. Llôlan travelled north-eastwards, and a tiny chapel at Broughton, 8 miles south-west of Peebles in the Scottish Borders, is named after him; it was excavated and roofed in the 1920s. The footings of its walls can be seen, with an arch set low in the present wall; presumably the original floor level was lower. This is one of the few chapels to survive from early times. Broughton Fair was held on Llôlan's feast day, 22 September, as late as 1864.

*Interior of Llôlan's chapel, Broughton.*

Broughton is on the A701 between Biggar and Peebles. To find the chapel, drive north on the A701, enter the village and pass the B7016 on your left. Stop at the village store on your left, and ask for the key to St Llôlan's Cell in the cemetery. Continue to the next exit left. As you turn into it, you will see the old church and cemetery up a lane, through a gate, on the right. The chapel, with its turfed roof, is near the church.

Llôlan became bishop of Whithorn. His staff and bell were preserved at Kinkardine church until the seventeenth century; the staff no longer survives, but Llôlan's bell may be the Celtic hand bell in the Glasgow Museums collection.

## Madern

Madern gave his name to the village of Madron in the moorland a mile north-west of Penzance. Even today, Maddern is a common surname in the village. Although it is only a small settlement today, Madron was the mother church of Penzance. An inscribed stone of fine whiteish granite in the church vestry provides a glimpse of the early community who worshipped here. Originally a pre-Christian standing stone, it was reused in the sixth or seventh century to mark a Christian burial. Its inscription suggests that a warrior or nobleman's widow commissioned it for her late husband, who was named 'Fair Slayer'. Above the inscription, the stonemason carved a simple trefoil cross. Displayed on a wall inside the church is a collection of tin marks, dating from 1189 onwards, carved with the *Agnus Dei* ('the Lamb of God') and seals of local families. In the churchyard are two small granite crosses, one bearing a simple figure of Christ.

Madern's well is one of Cornwall's most ancient and famous holy wells. It can be found by driving north through the village. Turn right after half a mile. The well is 10 minutes' walk along a signed track to the right. It is a small rectangular basin at ground level, overhung by ancient sallow willow trees. Tied to their branches are hundreds of clouties. This pre-Christian custom, still practised across Europe, Asia, Africa and South America, is a way of praying for healing or giving thanks for a cure.

The water flows into Madern's baptistery, 75m further along the track. There are the foundations of a solid twelfth-century building with a granite altar and a

*Early baptistery, Madron.*

baptismal basin built into its south-west corner. It was partially demolished at the time of the Reformation, and seventeenth-century observers noted a great thorn tree, whose branches formed a leafy roof over the chapel. Each year, parishioners used turf to repair a green bank alongside the altar, which they called 'St Madern's Bed'. Sick people came to bathe in the well and sleep on the bed, and many of them were cured, including a cripple who recovered so completely that he later enlisted in the Royalist army and was killed in action at Lyme Regis in Dorset in 1644. In 1750 the water from Madron well was channelled down the long hill to form the first water supply for Penzance.

## Maedoc of Ferns

Maedoc (a pet name meaning 'My little Aidan') was a sixth-century prince monk born in Connacht and educated in Leinster. He studied with Finnian of Clonard, and is said to have established a number of churches in the Irish kingdom of Kinsella, which corresponds roughly with the present diocese of Ferns. He also founded monasteries at Drumlane and Rossinver, both of which claim to be the site of his burial; he died in around 626. His late *Lives* are unreliable; one of them recounts that he bequeathed his staff, his bell and a reliquary to these three foundations. His staff survives in the National Museum, Dublin; his bell and reliquary can be found in Armagh cathedral library. The second Irish *Life of Maedoc of Ferns* states that when a King of Breifne was inaugurated, his wand or sceptre was to be cut from the hazel tree beside Maedoc's hermitage.

In 598 Bran Dubh, King of Leinster, gained a victory at the Battle of Dunboyke and, in gratitude for Maedoc's assistance, gave him land for a monastery at the royal seat of Ferns, 19 miles north of Wexford. Its name may come from the Gaelic for 'a place abounding in alders'. The extent of the enclosure's rampart may be indicated by the semi-circular wall which bounds part of the ancient graveyard beside Ferns cathedral. Maedoc was the principal bishop of Leinster for about 40 years; one of his successors was Moling, who is said to have named the well at Ferns in honour of

*View down into St Maedoc's well, Ferns.*

its founder. Maedoc's well lies across the road from the cathedral, a little further down the hill. It is very deep and was arched over in 1847. The spring water flows through a conduit into a stone trough beside the path that leads to the well.

In 787 the cathedral was referred to as 'the stone church of Ferns', at a time when building in stone was still rare. It became the burial place of the kings of Leinster; there are the remains of three high crosses in the graveyard. During the ninth and tenth centuries, the city and its cathedral were ravaged by the Irish and by the Danes, who plundered the church six times. In 1154 Dermot McMurrough, the last king of Leinster, burned the city and monastery, but rebuilt the church in 1169 as an abbey for Augustinian canons. He died in 1171 and asked to be buried 'near the shrines of St Mogue and St Moling' at Ferns; the name Mogue is a variant form of Maedoc. Parts of the present cathedral date from 1223–43, when the first Anglo-Norman bishop rebuilt it; the rest is more recent. Nearby, a ruined thirteenth-century building may have been the parish church.

## Mael: see Sulien

## Máelrubha

An Irishman who worked among the northern Picts, Máelrubha (c. 642–c. 722) became a monk at Bangor in County Down. He sailed to Scotland and established a flourishing monastery at Applecross, on the mainland opposite the Isle of Skye. He built a church on an island in Loch Maree, 35 miles west of Inverness, where his spring was famous for its healing properties. Máelrubha was killed by Norsemen at Skail, near the north coast of Sutherland. His body was brought back to his community at Applecross, but within a century the monastery had been destroyed by Vikings.

There are a number of dedications to Máelrubha on the Scottish west coast, including a church in the hamlet of Kilmory on the Knapdale peninsula, 2 miles north of the Point of Knap, facing the island of Jura. Kilmory is 14 miles south-west of Lochgilphead, and is reached by a minor road which runs through Knapdale Forest

*MacMillan cross, Kilmory, Knapdale peninsula.*

and along the east side of Loch Sween. Kilmory means 'cell of St Mary', but the small church was originally dedicated to Máelrubha.

The church dates from the early thirteenth century. It houses some early Christian decorated crosses, and later ones carved, like those found at other churches in the region, by Irish sculptors from Iona. Later, they travelled throughout Argyll with their pattern books, and local masons continued designing works in the same style until the mid sixteenth century. Their work is plentiful in this locality because much of the stone for the West Highland crosses was quarried beside nearby Loch Sween. Kilmory church houses the MacMillan cross, which was created in the fourteenth century, but executed in twelfth-century Romanesque style. It is an elaborate wheel cross with a figure of the crucified Christ at its centre.

# Maildubh

The name Maildubh may mean 'Black Prince'. According to medieval tradition, Maildubh was an Irish monk who established a small community and a school for noblemen's sons at Malmesbury. The Saxon monk Aldhelm (639–709) was his most outstanding pupil and became his successor. However, Aldhelm makes no mention of Maildubh in his prose works or poetry, and we hear nothing of the Irish monk until 400 years after Aldhelm's death.

The earliest histories of Malmesbury are those of Faricius of Arezzo (d. 1117), who lived at Malmesbury between 1080 and 1100 when he was appointed abbot of Abingdon, and by William of Malmesbury (c. 1090–1143). William describes Maildubh as an 'Irishman by birth, a philosopher by erudition and a monk by profession', who left Ireland in search of a solitary life. Although historians have cast doubt on Maildubh's existence, his story is not unlikely. Aldhelm himself tells us little about his own life, and nothing about his early education. William of Malmesbury notes that, on account of Viking raids, the abbey library lacked information about Aldhelm, so William's account was written largely from oral history.

Malmesbury is an ancient settlement. In 2000 a previously unknown Iron Age town was discovered beneath modern Malmesbury. It was 40 acres in size, and encircled by stone ramparts over 3m wide. The town was built between the fifth and second centuries BC, and was strongly fortified. The settlement was probably the main centre of a tribal group that eventually federated with its neighbours to become the kingdom of the Dobunni.

The Iron Age town was built on high ground within a loop of the River Avon, with a few hundred inhabitants sheltering behind 1.5m of stone defences. They lived in roundhouses of stone or timber, with roofs of thatch. They farmed, and the settlement was perhaps the chief economic centre of the south-east Cotswolds. Radiating out from it is a 30-mile cluster of Iron Age farms and settlements, as aerial photography shows.

The medieval town wall partly follows that of its Iron Age predecessor. Although Malmesbury stopped being a significant centre of population from about 100 BC to AD 800, it may have continued as a religious centre. There was possibly a small Romano-British temple beneath the abbey, dedicated to a local deity. This would be an obvious place for Christian monks to establish a community and a centre of learning.

The Saxons conquered this area in the sixth century, after a victory at Dyrham near Bath, and Malmesbury became part of the kingdom of the West Saxons. Aldhelm became abbot of Malmesbury in about 675; the south porch of the abbey may survive from his seventh-century church. Over the door, the tympanum depicts Christ enthroned, with supporting angels. Each side wall contains a panel of six apostles with an angel flying overhead. The rest of the south porch, with its bands of stone carving, dates from the twelfth or thirteenth century; it is one of the finest in Europe.

*Panel depicting six apostles, Malmesbury abbey porch.*

# Manchán

Twelve miles east of the great monastery of Clonmacnoise, on a small island rising out of a bog, a monk named Manchán established a hermitage in the early seventh century. The site is named Lemanaghan, or 'Manchán's grey place'. In 645, Manchán's patron, Diarmuid, King of Ireland, passed through Clonmacnoise when he marched to battle against Guaire, King of Connacht. The congregation of Clonmacnoise prayed to St Ciarán for King Diarmuid's safe return, and when he won the battle, he is said to have given the people Lemanaghan in memory of his victory. Both Manchán and Diarmuid died in the great plague of 664–66.

Lemanaghan is on the R436, between Clonmacnoise and Tullamore. The former island in the bog is now a low mound on which are remains of two Romanesque churches and six early grave slabs. Manchán is said to have settled here with his mother, Mella; a small stone oratory is known as her cell. At the lower end of the site, a short track leads to Manchán's well, which is approached down a flight of stone steps. Near the well is an ancient ash tree with knotted roots and branches to which local people tie clouties. Beside the well is a bullaun stone, a large stone with a cavity containing water, a feature of many early monastic sites. It may have been used for washing or perhaps its water was blessed and used in worship.

Manchán's magnificent shrine was recovered from the bog, together with part of an eleventh-century abbot's crosier; the shrine is now displayed in the nearby Catholic church at Boher. It was made around 1130 and contains a number of bones, believed to be Manchán's. It is constructed of yew wood in the shape of a gabled box 48cm high. It represents a house for the dead, and is lavishly decorated with cast

*Bullaun stone, containing water, Lemanaghan.*

gilt bronze and red and yellow fittings. The shrine is ornamented on either side with an elaborate metal cross, each having five prominent bosses. Around the crosses stood 50 elongated human figures, 11 of which have survived. There are intertwined beasts and serpents at the corners and at each end of the shrine, carved in an Irish version of a late Scandinavian style. During processions, the shrine was carried on a pair of wooden poles, threaded through rings mounted at each corner. This is the largest and most magnificent shrine to have been found in Ireland. If the church is locked, the key can be obtained from the presbytery to the right of the church.

## Maolcethair

A mile north of Gallarus Oratory, near the western end of the Dingle peninsula in County Kerry, Kilmalkedar is one of the few sites in the area which was not taken over by the cult of Brendan; it is dedicated to a local saint of the Corra Dhuibhne named Maolcethair, who died around 636; he may have been an Ulster prince. Kilmalkedar (or *Cill Mhaoilchédair* in Gaelic) means 'Church of Maolcethair'. The present church is twelfth-century Romanesque, with arcading modelled on Cormac's chapel at Cashel. On its roof a finial survives at the apex of the gable (see *colour plate 10*). There are considerable earlier remains from Maolcethair's monastery: to the west of the church,

along its ancient causeway, is the graveyard with a simple high cross. At the churchyard entrance is an ogham-inscribed stone and there are remains of a cell and also a finely carved sundial, with a hole into which the gnomon could be inserted. A sundial was important for monks with an organised day of work and prayer. An early eighth-century pillar stone inside the church has the Latin alphabet carved on it and was probably used to teach literacy to students.

*Celtic sundial, St Maolcethair's church, Kilmalkedar.*

# Materiana

Materiana may have been a Welsh princess. In medieval times, Minster church on the north Cornish coast contained her shrine. Minster was the mother church of Boscastle and it is set deep in a secluded wooded valley. An earlier name for Minster was Tolcarne or Talkarn, meaning a rocky chapel or cell. A church was built here in 1150 by William de Bottreaux, Lord of the Manor of Boscastle (or 'Bottreaux Castle'). The Norman tub font dates from this time; it is carved from porphyry stone and decorated with diagonal patterns. Porphyry is a hard rock composed of crystals of feldspar, which is a mineral containing aluminium and other silicates. Their tiny flecks gleam in the sunlight: this would have been a costly gift to Materiana's shrine.

The church was given to Benedictine monks from Anjou, in William's native France. A priory adjoined the church to the north; it is now destroyed. The monks lived here until about 1402, when King Henry IV closed all non-British monasteries. The church was restored in the sixteenth century and again in the nineteenth. On the terrace below the church there is a holy well, now dry. Minster was also the mother church of St Materiana's church in Tintagel. Minster is not marked on most maps; to find it, take the Tintagel road from the centre of Boscastle. At the top of the hill, bear left past the garage. Then take the second left. The church is a mile further on, in the valley below, on the left.

Materiana's relics were preserved at Minster until the Reformation. Her church at Tintagel is built within the dynastic cemetery of the fifth- and sixth-century chieftains who lived in the fort above the church. The present church dates from the eleventh to the fourteenth centuries.

*Norman font of porphyry, Minster.*

# Maughold

A church honours St Maughold, or Machaldus, at Kirk Maughold, on the north-east coast of the Isle of Man, on a hillside above the sea. There was a powerful spring at the site, and Norsemen may have named the place *Makt-kelda*, meaning 'forceful spring'. In his *Life of Patrick* (c. 1186), a monk named Jocelyn from the Benedictine abbey of Furness described the spring as St Machaldus' well. He linked it with the story of an Irish adventurer told by the seventh-century biographer of Patrick, Muirchú, who described a cruel tyrant named Macc Cuill and his dramatic conversion to a holy life. Macc Cuill normally killed travellers passing through his territory, and when he heard that Patrick was coming, he planned to murder him. Patrick survived and restored a dead man to life.

The tyrant was converted, declared his belief in God, confessed his sins and asked to do penance. Patrick ordered him to abandon everything and set off in a small boat without oars or a rudder. Macc Cuill was set adrift and arrived at a distant land, where two holy bishops trained him; eventually he too became a bishop. By telling the story of how a wicked man became a fervent monk, Muirchú presented a model of holy living. It was based on earlier moral tales: Cassian recounts how one of the Desert Fathers, Abba Moses, began as a murderer but was converted and became a wise and holy monk. It is considered unlikely, however, that there was a Manx saint named Maughold

Within the graveyard at Maughold are the remains of three early *keeills*, or chapels, and the sites of three more, including two beneath the medieval church. Each had a window of red sandstone and was surrounded by a small cemetery. The foundations of one *keeill* can be seen in the photograph, with a later well at its south-east corner. Maughold was the principal monastery on the Isle of Man. Its first monks appear to have originated from Northumbria and from

*Keeill at Maughold monastery.*

Galloway in south-west Scotland. The buildings were probably of timber, like those of Northumbrian monasteries. Many of its monuments were carved by itinerant Anglian stonemasons. Iron ore was mined at Maughold, which enabled metalworking to be carried out.

We gain glimpses of the monks who lived at the monastery from its fine collection of carved stone slabs. The oldest is a memorial to Irneit, a seventh-century monastic bishop. His name is inscribed in a circle surrounding a hexafoil cross. This design, resembling a six-petal flower, is found in sub-Roman Britain and Gaul, so the stonemason had learnt his skill abroad. A pair of eighth-century stones from the head and foot of a grave commemorate someone called Blakman. His name is Saxon, but the style of the cross is Celtic. It shows how Teutonic settlers spread across northern Britain and adopted Celtic culture.

Another slab is inscribed in Latin: 'Branhui led off water to this place.' Branhui was a monk with a Welsh name who provided the monastery with its water supply in about 800; traces of his stone-lined conduit have been found. An early ninth-century cross names a Welsh prince, Guriat, who may have taken refuge on the island before 825. Another cross from the same period depicts two Desert Fathers who inspired Celtic monks: St Antony and Paul the Hermit. They sit on solid chairs on either side of a ringed cross, each bearded and dressed in a monk's cowl and hood.

By 795 Vikings had begun to rob exposed places on the coast, and Maughold was an easy target. In around 830 colonists arrived and took possession of the arable land. Without land, the monastery could not continue; for a long period, no further monuments were constructed here. Norsemen buried their dead in the cemetery, for graves contain their weapons, including a sword dating from about 900. The present church dates from the twelfth century.

## Mawgan

Mawgan was a Welsh monk who is commemorated in a number of places, particularly in the Teifi valley, but no medieval life of him survives. In his eleventh-century *Life of David*, Rhigyfarch mentions a 'monastery of Maucannus', but whether or where it existed is uncertain. In Cornwall, two early sites are named after Mawgan: St Mawgan-in-Meneage and St Mawgan-in-Pydar. The beautiful Vale of Mawgan is 5 miles north-east of Newquay, with its ancient harbour of Mawgan Porth and its inland settlement of St Mawgan-in-Pydar. 'Pydar' is a Cornish word meaning 'hundred' – it denotes one of the six land divisions or 'hundreds' of Cornwall, and was an area which could produce 100 fighting men. Excavations at Mawgan Porth (1950–54) revealed three or four clusters of rectangular buildings, dating from about 850 to around 1050. Their occupants were farmers and fishermen with no metal implements. They kept sheep, goats, horses, oxen, dogs, cats and poultry. There was evidence of some contact with Anglo-Saxons: a coin from the time of Ethelred II (*c.* 1000) was found. Above the village was a cemetery of slate cist (or slab-lined) graves; the western part was set aside for many child burials. The site has been preserved on the sloping green opposite the beach, where the outline of some of the homes can be seen.

*St Mawgan-in-Pydar church and well.*

The soil near the shore was perhaps too barren to sustain a community of monks, but 2 miles up the river, where the land is more fertile, there was a Celtic monastery at St Mawgan-in-Pydar. The large parish church contains a fine Norman font. In the churchyard are two Cornish crosses, brought from elsewhere. Immediately inside the lychgate is the well, now dry, where Mawgan is said to have preached and to have baptised converts. Over the churchyard wall, outside the convent church of Lanherne, is a fine tenth-century cross carved by Runhol, who inscribed his name at its base. His name can be found on similar crosses at Sancreed and St Buryan.

Another Cornish village dedicated to Mawgan is St Mawgan-in-Meneage, at the northern tip of the Lizard, 4 miles south-east of Helston. 'Meneage' means 'land of the monks'. Mawgan Cross is an early grave marker on the village green, at a point where three roads meet. The stone dates from about 600, and is inscribed to 'Cnegumus, son of Genaius'. It stands 1.9m high. A cross head was later added to it, though it no longer exists. Setting sail from nearby Mawgan Creek, pilgrims could continue to north-east Brittany, where the saint is honoured in the region around St Malo.

# Melangell

According to legend, Melangell was an Irish chieftain's daughter who fled to Wales to escape an arranged marriage. She settled as a hermit at Pennant Melangell. A local chieftain named Brochwel, King of Powys, who lived in Shrewsbury, was hare coursing at Pennant Melangell. His hounds raised a hare which fled to a thicket where Melangell was praying. The hare hid in the folds of her cloak, while the hounds ran away. The huntsman raised his horn to his lips, but was unable to remove it. Brochwel was so impressed that he gave Melangell the valley, where she established a community of nuns. The remains of her shrine can be seen in the small church at Pennant Melangell, near the site of her grave.

The church of Melangell is at the head of a remote valley in the Berwyn Mountains of mid Wales. It is situated 20 miles west of Oswestry and 2 miles west of Llangynog. The churchyard had long been a holy place, and may be the burial site of a Bronze Age chieftain. It is encircled by ancient yew trees, perhaps dating

*Melangell's shrine, Pennant Melangell.*

from pre-Christian times. A cist grave lies beneath the stone floor of the tiny twelfth-century apse of Melangell's chapel; she may have been buried here before her remains were exhumed for veneration. A solid Norman font survives and Melangell's finely carved shrine, built in about 1164, has been sensitively restored.

Carved on the fifteenth-century rood screen, the prince, with his huntsman and hounds which feature in her story, chase a hare into Melangell's lap. A quarter of a mile south of her chapel, rock steps in the valley side lead to a ledge known as 'Melangell's Bed'. To find Pennant Melangell, drive to Llangynog. As the B4391 passes the church, turn sharply up a signed single-track road to the head of the valley, until the road ends at the shrine. The church is open daily.

## Melor: see Mylor

## Mirrin

In about 560 an Irish monk named Mirrin founded a community at Paisley on a tributary of the River Clyde, west of Glasgow. As a boy, Mirrin had been taken by his mother to Congal, the abbot of Bangor, a monastery at the head of Belfast Lough in Northern Ireland. After training as a monk, Mirrin became prior of Bangor and later went to Scotland, possibly as one of Columba's followers. On Inchmurrin ('Mirrin's Isle') in Loch Lomond, the largest island in the loch, a ruined chapel is dedicated to Mirrin; this was perhaps the site of a hermitage of Mirrin or one of his followers.

The ancient church of Paisley, close to present-day Glasgow airport, was built beside the White Cart River. The name Paisley may come from the Latin word 'basilica', meaning a church, so this may have been a Roman Christian settlement. There was a pre-Christian cemetery on the site, overlaid by the graves of Christians buried facing east. Excavation has provided evidence of a stone chapel and enclosure wall dating from the seventh or eighth century.

*Fifteenth-century stone frieze depicting scenes from Mirrin's life, Paisley Abbey.*

In medieval times, pilgrims visited Mirrin's shrine, and in the twelfth century Benedictine monks from Much Wenlock in Shropshire, which was a daughter house of Cluny, were brought to Paisley. A fifteenth-century stone frieze in Paisley abbey church illustrates scenes from Mirrin's life: a panel portrays him as prior of Bangor monastery; the central panel in the photograph depicts Mirrin praying in his cell at night, illuminated by a ray of heavenly light. The lowest section shows him reviving a monk who had died of heatstroke while working in the fields.

The abbey was founded in 1163 by the High Steward of Scotland. The fifth High Steward supported Scottish independence, and so the English set fire to the complex in 1307. The seventh High Steward became the first Royal Stewart, from whom Queen Elizabeth II is descended. There are extensive remains of the Cluniac monastery, including a vaulted chamber containing the main drain, constructed in about 1350. The abbey was largely rebuilt in the fifteenth century. A slate survives from its choir school, with the earliest surviving Scottish polyphonic music scratched on it, dating from around 1450.

## Mochta

Mochta was a disciple of Patrick who settled with some followers in Meath. It was said that after several years, because of local opposition, Mochta moved north to Louth, where he founded a large monastery and became its first bishop; he died in the sixth century. St Mochta's House (*Teach Naomh Mochta*) is found in the village of Louth, whose name derives from Lugh, the Celtic sun god. Situated 7 miles west of the Irish Sea coast and 7 miles north of Ardee, Louth was formerly so important that it gave its name to County Louth. St Mochta's House is a small church, probably built in the twelfth century. It is a fine example of a style of building unique to Ireland: a vaulted two-storeyed oratory with a roof croft over a barrel vault. The stone roof is supported by the arched vault beneath it, which prevents the building from falling inwards. A stairway leads to the upper floor, where a monk could sleep or study in the croft above the church.

Next to St Mochta's House is the ruined abbey of St Mary, thought to

*St Mochta's House, Louth.*

have been founded in 1148. Its fine west end dates from 1312, when it was rebuilt after a fire. Across the road, a wall indicates the site of the former twelfth-century abbey of Saints Peter and Paul, established in 1146. A section of the wall was known locally as 'the pinnacle', but the pinnacle collapsed within living memory. On the south side of the village is a mound on which stood a Norman motte, known as the Fairy Mount.

There is a ruined church of St Mochta in a field in the village of Rahan in County Offaly. It is situated 5 miles west of Tullamore, beside the River Brosna. A monastery was said to have been founded here by Mochta in the late sixth century; a new community was established on the site in about 760. There are the remains of the transept of a twelfth-century church; it was cruciform and had a fine round window. The church was altered in the fifteenth century and rebuilt in 1732. A second church was built in the twelfth century; its wall curves inwards to support a barrel-vaulted roof. A third ruined church stands in the graveyard at the other end of the field.

# Moling

The cult of Moling (d. 697) was early and widespread. Moling came from a noble Leinster family, and became a monk at Glendalough. He later founded his own monastery at St Mullins, beside the River Barrow in County Carlow. Moling is said to have established a ferry across the River Barrow; it is still in existence. He lived for a time in a hermitage near St Mullins, and later became bishop of Ferns, which lies to the east, over the Blackmore Mountains. Here he is said to have helped the people by obtaining the remission of a heavy

*Early church, 2.5m long, St Mullins.*

tribute of oxen to the local king. Moling was buried in the monastery of St Mullins. The base of a round tower can still be seen at the site, as can the remains of a small early church, 2.5m long. The upper portion of a high cross also survives, carved in granite in the ninth or tenth century, with a crucifixion scene.

On the opposite bank of the river is Moling's holy well. The water passes through a large pool into a well chapel, before flowing down to the river. In about 1160, Moling's monastery was annexed to the abbey of Augustinian canons at Ferns. The canons were responsible for building the six medieval churches, now in ruins, which dominate St Mullins; they may also have built St Moling's Mill. There is a small pocket gospel book in Trinity College, Dublin, named *The Book of Mulling*. It is encased in an elaborate jewelled shrine of bronze with silver plates, and was probably written in the ninth century, copied from a manuscript written by Moling. It contains the gospels, a Mass for the sick and a simplified plan of the monastery at St Mullins, whose boundary wall is indicated by two concentric circles. Twelve crosses are marked on the plan, but no buildings. This indicates that, symbolically at least, high crosses were a significant feature of Irish monastic life.

The small town of Llanfyllin in mid Wales, 18 miles west-north-west of Shrewsbury, is dedicated to Moling, and was possibly founded by one of his followers. The church was rebuilt in red brick in 1710. On the hillside 300m above the church is Moling's well. Its large chamber could be used for baptism by immersion. An account of 1894 describes how people tied rags to branches beside the spring as prayers for healing. On Trinity Sunday they came to drink sugared water at the well. The water was drawn by the girls, after which the lads paid for cakes and ale at the inn.

This was a survival from a medieval pilgrimage to the well, around the time of Moling's feast in June. Sugar water or liquorice water was often made at wells to improve the flavour of mineral-rich healing waters, and to symbolise life's sweetness. Sweetened water was also considered to be a tonic. To find the well, with the church on your left, continue along the main street. Soon there is a sign to turn right for the well. Turn up this street, and turn right again at the top. Continue up the hill, park, and continue on foot for another 100 yards. As the track bends to the left, the well is on the right, beneath a great sycamore tree.

# Moluag

Moluag was a sixth-century monk from Bangor monastery in north-east Ireland who sailed to Scotland and founded a community on the island of Lismore. He was a contemporary of Columba, but his followers worked independently of Iona. From Lismore, churches were later established in eastern Scotland, Skye and the Outer Hebrides. His pastoral staff of blackthorn survives, enshrined in gilded copper.

Moluag's church, at the Butt of Lewis in the Outer Hebrides, is situated at the northernmost point of the island. It stands in a field 250 yards north of Eorpaidh village, and was founded or re-established on a Celtic site at the end of the twelfth century by a Norse or Norse-Celtic chieftain in Lewis. Its plan, with small side chapels near the eastern end is typical of twelfth- and thirteenth-century

# THE SAINTS

*St Moluag's cathedral, Eorpaidh, Isle of Lewis.*

early Norse architecture. The putlog holes in the walls also date from this period (these held timbers to which scaffolding was tied during the construction of the church). In Norse times, the church was dedicated to St Olaf. Locally it is known as 'the cathedral', and people with injured limbs brought or sent a wooden replica of their wounded limb to the church to be laid on the altar, in order to be cured by St Moluag.

## Mungo: see Kentigern

## Mylor

The settlement of Mylor in Cornwall is probably named after one of two or three Breton saints named Melor. The cult of Mylor or Melor was centred on the church of Lanmeur near Morlaix in Finistère, an area of western Brittany. Here he was believed to have been a prince who was murdered. Mylor's cult probably spread to Cornwall from Brittany. Two miles north of Falmouth as the crow flies, Mylor is one of a number of Celtic sites around the Fal estuary which are most easily reached from the sea. The church stands above the harbour, on an early site. As with other Celtic foundations such as Golant and St Just in Roseland, the church is situated just above the main seaway, out of sight of pirates. The farmhouse beside the vicarage is called Lawithick, or 'church site among the trees'; the use of the (abbreviated) prefix *lan* denotes an early foundation. East of the south porch, an unusual granite cross stands 5m high. This was a pre-Christian monolith, with a sun symbol consisting of three concentric circles carved at its top; the stone is taller than it appears, for it is planted 2m deep. It was later capped

*St Mylor's well, Linkinhorne.*

with a Christian cross. Water from the well in the churchyard is still used for christenings and the spring flows into a small brook.

Linkinhorne in eastern Cornwall is also dedicated to Mylor. Amesbury abbey acquired his relics at the time of its foundation in about 979, and Mylor became a patron saint of the abbey.

*Right: Former chapel beside Nectan's Kieve, Bossiney.*

## Nectan

Claimed to be the eldest of Brychan's 24 children, Nectan's legendary life is known from three twelfth-century documents written at Hartland abbey in Devon: a short *Life*, an account of the rediscovery of his relics and a list of his miracles. Nectan is not mentioned in Welsh accounts of Brychan, although a monk named Nectan occurs in medieval Welsh genealogies. The *Life* relates that Nectan crossed the Bristol Channel and settled at Stoke in Hartland as a hermit. His brothers and sisters settled in Wales, Devon and Cornwall, and met together at his cell every New Year's Eve; in this way, the monks of Hartland claimed authority for their foundation. Nectan was said to have been beheaded by two robbers; he was widely venerated in south-west Britain.

At Nectan's Kieve, a waterfall near Tintagel on the north Cornish coast, a medieval chapel may have been dedicated to him. A mile north-east of Tintagel, the River Trevillitt flows through woodland towards the sea at Bossiney. Half an hour's walk upstream leads to a waterfall known as Nectan's (or Nighton's) Kieve. *'Kieve'* is Cornish for 'bowl'; it describes the pool enclosed by rocks beneath the waterfall. At the top of the falls are the lower courses of what may have been a medieval chapel. Its walls are a metre thick; the timber superstructure was added in 1860. The local story is that Nectan lived as a hermit here, at the head of the glen.

# Neot

In his *Life of Alfred*, Bishop Asser (d. 910) writes that King Alfred visited a church in Cornwall 'in which St Guerin lies in peace (and now St Neot lies there as well)'. Neot appears to be a Celtic name, although later *Lives* claim that he was a Saxon or an East Anglian, to make his story more attractive to their respective readers. As a young man, Neot is said to have joined the community in Glastonbury and to have settled as a hermit at St Neot on Bodmin Moor in Cornwall, where he founded a community. His relics were enshrined here, although most of them were later taken to St Neots in Huntingdon and to Crowland abbey in Lincolnshire. Neot's legend is portrayed in 12 early sixteenth-century panels of stained glass in St Neot church, Cornwall. They represent incidents from the twelfth-century *Life of Neot*, written at Bec in Normandy, but these are borrowed from other *Lives* of Irish saints.

The village of St Neot is on the southern edge of Bodmin Moor, 5 miles north-west of Liskeard. It is mentioned in *Domesday Book* (1086), at which time there was a small community of monks at St Neot. The churchyard contains one of the finest Celtic crosses in Cornwall, carved of granite and richly ornamented with interlacing. It probably dates from the late ninth century; its style resembles that of King Doniert's Stone at St Cleer and others at Lanivet, Sancreed and Cardinham. Nearby are three wayside crosses brought from elsewhere in the parish and a fifteenth-century lantern cross from St Kew.

The church contains magnificent stained-glass windows dating from the fifteenth and sixteenth centuries. They tell the stories of saints

*Neot visits the Pope, from a stained-glass window in St Neot church.*

and angels, the Creation, the Flood and the life of St Neot. One window portrays a crowned figure with children in his lap. The nineteenth-century restorer has inserted an inscription which describes the figure as Brychan, although it is more likely to represent God the Father or Abraham with the souls of the righteous in his bosom.

St Neot's holy well is 400m from the church, near the St Neot River. To find it, leave the church and turn right along the main road. Turn right again, along a signed track, following the river. The well is in a field at the foot of a scarp. Michell in his *Parochial History of St Neots* (1833) states that 'there was an arch of stones over it, with a large oak springing from the arch, and with doors to the entrance. [It] was remembered by some old inhabitants of the village lately deceased ... Weakly children used within living memory to be brought here.' The well house was rebuilt in 1862. The name of the early settlement of Menheniot, 3 miles south-east of Liskeard, may mean 'sanctuary of Neot'.

# Ninian

We know very little about the early bishop Ninian except that he worked in Galloway, in south-west Scotland. Writing 300 years later, Bede tells us that Ninian studied in Rome before founding a monastery, which he dedicated to Martin of Tours (Bede's *Ecclesiastical History*, bk 3, ch. 4). Bede tells us how Ninian established a monastery at a place called *candida casa* (Latin for 'white, or shining, house'). In Old English this was translated as *hwit aern*, from which is derived the modern name of Whithorn. It has been suggested that Ninian originated from Carlisle, which was the centre of an early bishopric, and Whithorn is likely to have come within its ambit. A church probably existed in Carlisle from late Roman times onward, since fourth-century Christian artefacts have been found there.

The small town of Whithorn is near the coast, 40 miles south-west of Dumfries. Bede writes:

> The southern Picts, who dwell on this side of [the Grampian] mountains, had ... embraced the truth by the preaching of Ninian, a most pious bishop and holy man of the Britons, who had been regularly instructed at Rome in the faith and mysteries of the truth, whose episcopal see is named after St Martin the bishop, and is famous for a stately church (where he and many other saints are laid to rest). It is still in existence. The place belongs to the province of Bernicia, and is generally called the White House, because he there built a church of stone, which was not usual among the Britons.

A stone church suggests one built in the Roman or Continental style. Excavation has provided evidence of successive churches on the site dating from the sixth, seventh and eighth centuries. When Bede mentions St Martin the bishop, he is referring to Martin of Tours, who developed monastic life in Gaul after learning how monks lived in the Near East. Excavations conducted by Peter Hill yielded potsherds indicating contact with Europe over a long period: fragments from the Mediterranean dated around 500, Gaulish pieces from about 550 and Frankish and Gaulish plain ceramic ware from around 600. There were pieces of eight glass bowls from the eastern Mediterranean, or Spain or Rome, dating from the fifth or sixth centuries. There were also fragments of fine African red slipware imported from Carthage in the mid sixth century, and fragments of many agricultural tools, including a pebble-board plough (see *colour plate 12*).

A fine collection of inscribed stones can be seen in the small museum at the site. One is an early fifth-century memorial stone carved in a style developed in Gaul. It was erected for a man named Latinus by the descendants of Barrovadus, who may have been the local chieftain. It perhaps marked the gift of this site to the Church. Another monument, the 'Petrus Stone', formerly stood on high ground south-east of the monastery. It reveals traces of three different periods. First, a damaged, dressed face from an earlier inscription or design may have been removed. The violence of its removal suggests that it was no longer welcome. Second is a stemmed cross of arcs, dating from the seventh century. It is symmetrically placed and carefully executed. Finally, there is an irregularly placed inscription of three lines reading LOCI PETRI APUSTOLI. It proclaims the *locus*, or place, of Peter the Apostle. This can probably be attributed to the Northumbrians and reflects the popularity of St Peter following the triumph of the Roman party at the Council of Whitby. The stone may have stood beside the old road from Whithorn to the Isle of Whithorn, and was perhaps associated with a chapel.

The Anglo-Saxons established a bishopric at Whithorn, constructing a church and a large monastic complex. Today, wooden posts indicate the outline of the church, built in about 750, and two timber halls, which would have had bowed walls and curved, ridged roofs. The first Saxon bishop, Pecthelm, was a correspondent of both Bede and of Boniface, the English-born archbishop of Mainz. The Northumbrians popularised Ninian's cult to legitimise their control of the Britons in Galloway. One monk wrote a poem about Ninian's life and miracles, and sent a copy to the scholar Alcuin at Charlemagne's court. The Northumbrian thanked him and sent back a silk veil for Ninian's shrine. Below the chancel of the twelfth-century priory at Whithorn, excavations have revealed the stone coffins of Northumbrian clerics. Several fine carved crosses also date from this time, including the Petrus Stone.

In the twelfth century, King David I of Scotland brought the Scottish Church more fully under the control of Rome. He encouraged religious orders to take over native foundations, and Whithorn became a priory of Premonstratensian monks. The Cistercian Abbot Ailred of Rievaulx, who had been educated at King David's court, wrote a *Life of Ninian*. He had access to a now lost British *Life*, but he admits that he despised its 'barbarous language'. He describes Ninian carrying out centralising policies of which King David would approve: 'Then [Ninian] began to ordain priests, consecrate bishops, distribute other clerical honours and divide the whole land into parishes.' However, Ailred also travelled to Whithorn and collected stories about Ninian from the Galloway region, which then belonged to Ailred's own diocese of York.

Ninian is said to have used a cave as a quiet retreat. It is on the seashore 5 miles south-west of Whithorn, and is approached by an ancient path. Seven Celtic and Northumbrian crosses are carved on its walls; the earliest of these may pre-date the Northumbrian conquest of Galloway, which took place in about 730. This suggests

*St Trinian's chapel, Greeba, Isle of Man.*

that the cave soon became a place of pilgrimage. Three miles from the town on the opposite shore lies the Isle of Whithorn, which is now joined to the mainland. It was probably associated with the monastery throughout its history. There are traces of a Celtic fort on the island, around the ruins of a thirteenth-century chapel in which pilgrims arriving by sea could give thanks for their safe arrival.

A Manx and Scots Gaelic form of Ninian is Trinian, and there are several churches dedicated to Trinian in northern Scotland. Monks from Whithorn also settled on the Isle of Man, where the ruins of St Trinian's chapel can be seen beside the road from Douglas to Peel, south-east of Greeba. Whithorn was granted land near Greeba in the twelfth century, and the chapel's south door dates from this time. There was an earlier building on the site: a sixth- or seventh-century cross slab survives, while to the right of the altar, paving stones form a plain cross within a circle and may mark the site of the founder's shrine.

# Non

In his *Life of David*, written around 1095, Rhigyfarch tells us that David's father was Sant, King of Ceredigion, and his mother, from the neighbouring kingdom of Dyfed, was called Non. According to Rhigyfarch, she was a virgin who conceived her son through being raped by Sant when he was passing through Dyfed (modern Pembrokeshire). After the rape, Non lived on bread and water. It was seen as fitting that David's parents should be named Sant (from the Latin *sanctus* or 'holy') and Non, meaning 'nun'.

On a cliff top in St Non's Bay, a mile south of St David's cathedral, St Non's chapel is supposed to mark the spot where Non gave birth to David. The medieval chapel is built on Celtic foundations and the giant stones near the base of the building may date from this time. The building is oriented north to south, which would have been unusual for a chapel. Excavations carried out in the nineteenth century revealed slab-lined or 'cist' graves, probably dating from between the seventh and ninth centuries, to the east and south of the oratory. Inside, a gravestone carved with a simple ringed cross dates from the same period. Surrounding the chapel are giant Bronze Age boulders.

Close to Non's chapel is her holy well. This is one of the chief holy wells of Wales; it was famous for curing eye diseases. In the early eighteenth century, Browne Willis wrote:

> There is a fine well ... covered with a stone roof and enclosed within a wall, with benches to sit upon round the well. Some old, simple people go still to visit this saint ... especially upon St Nun's day (2 March), which they keep holy and offer pins, pebbles etc. at this well.

A century later, the well was still popular, as Fenton reported:

> The fame this consecrated spring had obtained is incredible, and still it is resorted to for many complaints. In my infancy ... I was often dipped in it, and offerings, however trifling, even a farthing or a pin, were made after each ablution, and the bottom of the well shone with votive brass.

In the field leading to the chapel, there was a house for the well's caretaker. The well house was restored in 1951. There is a modern retreat house nearby, and a chapel dedicated to Our Lady and St Non, built in 1934 in the medieval style.

Non's cult spread to Cornwall, where Pelynt and Altarnun may be named after her. Pelynt's name comes from *plou Nent*, which means 'parish of Non'. It is the only example of a Cornish church which incorporates the Breton word *plou*. This is an early loan word derived from the Latin *plebs*, meaning 'the people [of God]'. The church at Pelynt, 3 miles west of Looe, may stand within an Iron Age 'round', a circular settlement site. The Norman church was rebuilt in the fifteenth century.

Non's well is a mile down the valley in Hobb Park, where a spring emerges from the hillside. Although restored, the well house retains its original shape, with a curved roof, a stone lintel and walls of flat, unmortared stones. On either side of the entrance is a stone bench where pilgrims could sit and pray. Inside the well house, water trickles into a heavy bowl of pink granite, incised with wheel crosses; it dates from Celtic times.

A hundred years ago, the outline of a mound and wall could still be traced above the well; this appears to have been a chapel. The site may be linked with an Iron Age encampment further up the hill. To find the well, take either minor road east from Pelynt, down a steep hill to Watergate. Turn left into the road for Duloe. Before crossing the bridge over the West Looe River, bear left up a road signed 'Hobb Park'. Continue for a mile, and park at the cattle grid at the top of the hill. The well is signed in the first field on the right, down a flight of steps.

*St Non's well, Carnanton, Cornwall.*

Altarnun, meaning 'altar of Non', is 7 miles south-west of Launceston. This beautiful village grew up around a fast-flowing stream, a tributary of the River Inney, on the north-east side of Bodmin Moor. The church is on high ground above the medieval bridge; there is a solid Cornish cross in the churchyard. The church contains an elaborate twelfth-century font and there are traces of original painting on its carved faces. The four heads facing four directions symbolise, among other things, the four evangelists taking the good news of the gospel to the ends of the earth. Above the altar, medieval glass fragments may depict Non. There is a fine wooden rood screen and 79 bench ends carved between 1510 and 1531 by Robart Daye. They include musicians playing the medieval fiddle and the Cornish bagpipes, and some of the earliest carvings of corn dollies.

Non's holy well is in a field above the church, beside an ancient hawthorn tree. The well feeds a bowssening pool, which was used to cure insanity by a primitive form of shock therapy. Until the eighteenth century, insane people were tumbled into the pool by a sudden blow to the chest. They were tossed up and down, accompanied by the chanting of prayers, until they were exhausted. The patients were then taken down to the church, where Masses were sung for their recovery. There used to be a similar bowssening pool at St Cleer, 8 miles south of Altarnun. To find St Non's well, with the churchyard wall on your left, walk uphill along the road leading north-east out of Altarnun. Enter the second field on your right, by way of a track. The bowssening pool and hawthorn tree beside Non's well are now visible in a small enclosure on the right, across the corner of the field.

There is another Cornish well dedicated to Non at Carnanton near St Mawgan-in-Pydar. To find it, take the A3059 Newquay Road, signed 'Newquay Airport'. The well can be visited with permission; it can be found just past the third gate on the right signed 'private', where a small stream emerges from the bank inside the wood. In Brittany, Non is sometimes commemorated as a male companion of David. Non is said to have died in western Brittany and to be buried at Dirinon, 10 miles east of Brest.

# Padarn

Padarn was an early Welsh monk whose seven known dedications are beside two Roman roads which run north and south, linking forts on either side of the Cambrian Mountains. This may imply that Padarn's followers worked in the settlements around the ruined Roman garrisons of south Wales. His name, Paternus, was a common Roman name; he may have preceded David, who also has dedications in this area. His chief monastery was at Llanbadarn Fawr, now a southern suburb of Aberystwyth, on the Welsh coast.

According to medieval tradition, Padarn persuaded the local chieftain to give him land between the rivers Rheidol and Clarach, where he built Llanbadarn Fawr on a hillside. The site is near *Sarn Helen*, an ancient route continuing the line of the Roman coastal road and the trackway is named after Helen, the wife of Magnus Maximus. For 20 years, Padarn was bishop and abbot of the monastery at Llanbadarn Fawr. A pre-Christian standing stone carved into a cross can be seen in the church. There is also a narrow granite pillar cross, 3m high, carved in about 750, on which a worn figure with a crosier may represent Padarn.

Llanbadarn Fawr had close links with Ireland, and it may have become a reformed community reflecting the influence of the Irish *Céli Dé* (or 'Servants of God'), as did St David's and Seriol's monastery at Penmon. Unlike other Welsh monasteries in the south-west, Llanbadarn Fawr became a centre of learning. By the eleventh century, under Abbot Sulien the Wise, its library was larger than those of Canterbury cathedral or York Minster. Sulien was twice bishop of St David's; his four sons also became monks at Llanbadarn. The eldest, Rhigyfarch, wrote a *Life of David*. Another, Ieuan, later arch-priest of Llanbadarn, illustrated *Rhigyfarch's Psalter* and wrote a poem about his father Sulien, wistfully recalling the former greatness of the monastery, which by then had perhaps been absorbed into the sphere of influence of St David's.

*Pre-Christian standing stone carved into a cross, Llanbadarn Fawr.*

# Patrick

Patrick was a Briton who worked in Ireland in the fifth century; his father was a Roman *decurion*, or civic official. In his remarkable autobiography, the *Confession*, Patrick tells us that his father was a deacon and his grandfather was a priest. Patrick does not tell us where he was born; one possibility among others is the area of western Scotland near Dumbarton, in the Romanised area south of the Antonine Wall. In his *Confession*, which he wrote in old age, Patrick tells us that when he was 16 he was captured by Irish raiders and taken to Ireland as a slave. Put to work as a shepherd tending flocks, he began to pray and became converted to a monastic way of life. He recalls: 'I even remained in the wood and on the mountain to pray. And – come hail, rain or snow – I was up before dawn to pray ... I now understand this, that the Spirit was fervent in me' (*Confession*, 16).

After six years Patrick escaped or was freed and returned home to Britain. He trained as a priest, perhaps in Gaul. Patrick felt drawn to return to Ireland as a missionary and eventually did so. He tells us that he was a bishop, and he appears to have been based in the north-east, where he may have founded a settlement at Armagh. The later monks of Armagh claimed him as the founder of their cathedral, and they recorded stories about Patrick which may be based on fact or may simply be ecclesiastical propaganda to promote their patron saint.

Patrick's seventh-century biographer, Muirchú, describes a dramatic confrontation between the saint and the high king who lived at Tara, 25 miles north-west of Dublin. He relates how Easter that year fell on the same day as the great Celtic fire festival, when every fire had to be extinguished until a new one was lit on Tara at dawn. Patrick gathered his followers on the nearby hill of Slane, 12 miles further north, to celebrate the resurrection of Christ by lighting the Easter fire. The furious king came to Tara and encountered Patrick, who then emerged victorious from a contest of magic with the king's bards. Muirchú linked Patrick with Tara at a time when the church of Armagh was forging an alliance with the rising dynasty of the Uí Néill, who used the ancient capital of Tara as a symbol of their authority.

In his *Confession*, Patrick tells us that he travelled to the far ends of the known world in order to bring Christianity to an alien people. He established Christian communities and trained others to lead them. Patrick may have worked in central and northern Ireland, while other early bishops were preaching in the south. A story relates how Patrick came to Cashel to visit Aongus, King of Munster, who agreed to be baptised. During the ceremony, Patrick accidentally pierced the king's foot with his staff. The king made no complaint, thinking that this was part of the ritual.

As an old man, Patrick wrote two letters to the soldiers of Coroticus, who was possibly a chieftain living on Dumbarton Rock, capital of the British kingdom of Strathclyde. Dumbarton's fortified peaks tower above the Clyde estuary, and enemy armies or ships could be seen from a great distance. The second of Patrick's letters to Coroticus survives; in it we learn that the chieftain's soldiers had raided Ireland, captured some of Patrick's converts and sold them to the Picts, and that Patrick wrote demanding their release. We do not know where or how Patrick died. Many Irish churches claim to have been founded by Patrick and his followers.

*Dumbarton Rock, site of the fort of Coroticus, Strathclyde.*

Croagh Patrick in County Mayo is named St Patrick's Mountain, although it is unlikely to have been visited by Patrick, although it has been climbed by pilgrims since the twelfth century. Croagh Patrick is 763m high, and it is now the site of an annual pilgrimage held in Patrick's honour on the last Sunday in July. The mountain lies 6 miles west of Westport, and rises abruptly from the plain. It can be climbed from Murrisk on the R335, where there is a car park. A small road leads to a white statue of Patrick, from where a stony track continues. The final climb is up a steep slope covered with quartzite scree; the ascent is strenuous and takes two or three hours. As one climbs, there are magnificent views over Clew Bay to the north and Connemara to the south. There is a chapel on the flat top of the hill and many pilgrims shed their footwear before completing the final stage of their journey.

Another site which later became associated with Patrick is Lough Derg. Three miles south of Donegal, the R232 branches left off the N15 to Pettigo, from where the R233 leads north through desolate countryside to Lough Derg. In the lough lies Station Island, known in medieval times as St Patrick's Purgatory. Although there is no evidence that Patrick came here, every year large numbers of pilgrims visit the site; during the pilgrimage season, from June to August, no other visitors are allowed onto the island. A monk named Mobeoc or Dabeoc settled on one of the other islands in Lough Derg, *Oilean na Naomh* ('Saints' Island'), but nothing is known about him.

Lough Derg attracted pilgrims from across Europe from the late twelfth century onwards. The Augustinians established a community on Saints' Island and became responsible for the 'Purgatory' on nearby Station Island. The pilgrimage now lasts three days; each person must walk barefoot and eat only one daily meal, consisting of bread and black tea. Participants keep an all-night vigil in the modern basilica and say special prayers at the penitential 'beds' which are the footings of early monks' cells. There are modern hospices providing accommodation. St Patrick's Purgatory is known as 'the hardest pilgrimage in Christendom'.

## Paul Aurelian

Paul Aurelian was a prominent figure in Celtic times. We learn about him from a *Life* written in 884 by a monk named Wrmonoc at the Breton monastery of Landévennec in Finistère. The biographer conflated his story with one or possibly two other Pauls, but it seems that Paul Aurelian was born in Wales into an important Romano-British family in the late fifth century. The author tells us that, as a young man, Paul studied alongside David and Samson in Illtud's famous monastery at Llanilltud Fawr in south Wales. According to his biographer, Paul left Illtud's community at the age of 16 and became a hermit, living 'in the uninterrupted life of contemplation'. He founded a monastery at Llanddeusant near Llandovery, and was ordained as a priest. He left with 12 monks, after which he may have established a community at Llangors, near Brecon.

In time, Paul's fame reached the court of King Mark, who may have lived in the hill fort of Castle Dore, near Fowey on the south Cornish coast. His biographer tells us that Mark ruled over a people who spoke four languages, and he wished to strengthen their Christian faith. At his invitation, Paul arrived with 12 priests. He spent some time working there, but when he was asked to become their bishop he left and sailed to Brittany. Paul founded a church on the Île-de-Batz and agreed to become the first bishop of the settlement that was later named St-Pol-de-Léon in his honour; he was widely venerated in this area of Brittany.

It is possible that the parish of Paul near the south Cornish coast, 2 miles south of Penzance, was given its name by Breton monks who brought Paul Aurelian's cult to Cornwall. The church is at an ancient holy site, for built into the churchyard wall near the main gate is a large Neolithic standing stone, perhaps 4000 years old, capped with a Celtic cross. It stands beside the old road leading down to Mousehole harbour, which was an embarkation point for Brittany in early times. The large church at Paul was rebuilt in granite in the fifteenth century.

Llangors is a small town 6 miles east of Brecon in south-east Wales, in the foothills of the Black Mountains. The full name of the settlement was Llan yn y Gors, or 'church in the marsh'. It is dedicated to Paulinus, or Paul Aurelian, and two other chapels in the parish are named after him: Llanbeulin and Llan y Deuddeg Sant (or 'church of the twelve saints'), referring to the 12 monks who accompanied Paul Aurelian. It would have been appropriate for Paul to establish a community at Llangors, for this appears to have been the royal burial ground for the kings of Brycheiniog (now Brecon), who may have lived in the crannog in nearby Llangors Lake.

A charter of Llandaff, ostensibly from the eighth century, but probably tenth century in origin, states that King Awst of Brycheiniog and his sons gave a royal estate corresponding to the present parish of Llangors to Bishop Euddogwy. It records that King Awst requested that he and his sons might be buried in the church at Llangors. Another Llandaff charter tells of a meeting at the monastery in Llangors around 925 between King Tewdwr of Brycheiniog and Bishop Libiau, to settle a dispute over food rent. Inside Llangors church at the west end there is an inscribed gravestone dating from the sixth or seventh century and an early cross slab decorated with pockmark patterns. The font dates from about 1300. The present building dates from the fifteenth century and was restored in the nineteenth century. The key to the church can be obtained from the vicarage, which is set back from the road, behind the church.

Llangors Lake is half a mile south-east of the village and is the largest natural lake in south Wales. A crannog is situated 40m from the northern shore of the lake. This is an artificial island which today measures 40m across and is covered by trees and reeds. It was formerly occupied by buildings, which may have periodically housed the *llys*, or court, of the King of Brycheiniog. Manuscript B of the *Anglo-Saxon Chronicle* relates that shortly before midsummer in 916, the Saxon King Aethelflaed sent an army to Wales to destroy the palace on the lake; they captured the queen and 33 of the king's followers. In the 1190s, Gerald of Wales in his *Journey Through Wales* recorded a folk memory of the destruction of the island palace of Llangors. Local inhabitants said that there was a town beneath the waters of the lake; sometimes the city could be seen floating in the surface of the lake. They said that the lake sometimes turned bright green and occasionally scarlet.

A sixteenth-century manuscript reports that local people observed 'sometyme, greate peeces of tymber and fframes of houses ffleeting upon the water' (*De Mirabilibus Cambriae*, or 'The Wonders of Wales'). This refers to the remains of timber planks forming the crannog's palisade, which was then still prominent. The crannog was observed in the late 1860s by two local antiquarians, Edgar and Henry Dumbleton, after the lake level had been lowered. They described a substantial mound of boulders lying on top of brushwood, reeds and sand. They noted that the south and west sides of the mound were edged by one or two oak palisades.

*Llangors crannog, site of an early chieftain's palace.*

Prompted by these accounts, a team from the University of Wales, College of Cardiff excavated Llangors crannog in 1989-90. They concluded that the island had been periodically extended from an initial platform. Timber from earlier structures was incorporated into later ones. Dating of one sample gave a tree-ring sequence of AD 747-859, indicating construction in the ninth and early tenth centuries, 300 years before the Norman conquest of this part of Wales. In 1925 a log canoe had been found here, dated to around 800; it is now in the museum at Brecon. The crannog at Llangors is the only one to have been identified in England or Wales, although there are many in Scotland and Ireland. Crannogs were principally defensive in purpose. Most show gaps in their palisade, usually facing the shore, where boats could land. Some, like that at Llangors, were reached by a causeway. The occupants usually lived by farming around the lake shore and by fishing.

Crannogs were constructed by driving piles into the mud. The island was built up in layers of various available materials until it rose above the surface of the water. The name 'crannog' is derived from the Irish word *crann*, meaning a tree; this refers to the common use of timber in their construction. During the excavations of the 1880s, bone, charcoal and a few fragments of leather, pottery and metal were found. The excavations during 1989-90 recovered evidence of animal husbandry and cereal cultivation. Smelting was suggested by fragments of fired clay from furnace linings or hearths, and slag. A bone comb was found, as well as rare pieces of textile. The fine quality of its weave and the carefully planned construction of the entire site indicates that Llangors was the home of one of the leading families of ninth- and tenth-century Wales. The construction of the site required an ability to call upon a high level of specialised knowledge and resources.

## Petroc

Petroc was one of Cornwall's most popular saints in medieval times; his name may mean 'little Peter'. The earliest *Life of Petroc* survives in Breton manuscripts, but it was probably written by a Cornish cleric, since the author was familiar with various locations in Cornwall which were associated with him. The eleventh-century biographer tells us that Petroc was a Welsh prince who became a monk and went to Ireland to study with his companions. They returned to mainland Britain, and landed at Padstow on the north Cornish coast in Cornwall; the town's name means 'Petroc's stow'.

Padstow parish church was believed to be the site of his burial. Set into the wall to the right of the altar in the late medieval church, there is a carving of a monk which possibly represents Petroc or may be St Antony (see *colour plate 5*). He is bearded and holds a walking stick and a hand bell, with which to summon people to pray. He also holds a book of the gospels, for he preaches the word of God. The statue was probably preserved from an earlier church on the site, where it might have stood in a niche above the church porch for worshippers to see as they entered the building. Outside the porch is a tall Celtic cross. In the church there is a fine fourteenth-century font, carved in black catacleuse stone from a nearby quarry, between Mother Ivey's and Harlyn Bay. Around the bowl of the font, 12 apostles are depicted, with an angel at each corner.

In the late tenth century, Petroc's shrine with his staff and his bell were taken inland to Bodmin, perhaps because of Viking raids around the coast. Augustinian canons encouraged Bodmin's development as a centre for pilgrimage to Petroc's shrine. In the late twelfth century, a canon of Bodmin priory wrote a longer *Life of Petroc*, linking him with Welsh traditions. He relates how Petroc travelled inland with his companions to a remote location where a hermit named Guron lived. The writer is describing his own priory of Bodmin. He tells of the monk's arrival at Bodmin, where Guron welcomed Petroc and his three companions hospitably, setting out a table with white bread for them.

Guron left them his hut, and travelled a day's journey to Gorran, near the Cornish coast, 7 miles south of St Austell. This village was the centre of Guron's cult. Although Guron is, in fact, more likely to have been a chieftain than a hermit, medieval tradition incorporated him into Petroc's story. Dwarfed by the splendid minster church of Bodmin is the hermit's well, in a sixteenth-century well house. Above its entrance is a relief of Guron kneeling beneath a tree. He prays before a crucifix carved over the door of his cell. The well is now dry; the spring has been channelled through pipes and a great volume of water now pours into a trough beside the main street, below the well.

Little Petherick (or 'Petroc's little settlement') is also associated with Petroc. The canon of Bodmin priory who wrote the late twelfth-century *Life of Petroc* describes the abbot appointing a deputy to take charge of his monastery in Padstow, and then leaving with 12 companions to live in a nearby wilderness: a tidal creek in the estuary of the River Camel, named Nansfonteyn, or 'valley with a spring'. The creek of Little Petherick, 2 miles south of the busy town of Padstow, is still a tranquil place. Here, according to the Bodmin canon, Petroc built a chapel and a mill. He lived on 'bread and water, with porridge on Sundays'. The author describes Petroc practising

*Petroc's twelfth-century head reliquary, Bodmin.*

the austere life traditional among Irish monks: he immerses himself in the creek up to his neck, chanting the psalms. Petroc's church is built into the hillside. Four pinnacles that decorate its tower were brought from a ruined chapel dedicated to Cadoc, in nearby Harlyn Bay. A short walk along the tributary of the Camel leads to Petroc's well, in a garden to the left of the track. The spring's course has altered and the water now tumbles past the dry well house.

The Bodmin canon relates that Petroc ended his days as a hermit on the bleak open spaces of Bodmin Moor. His head reliquary can be seen in Bodmin church, which was constructed by Arab craftsmen in Sicily in the twelfth century. It is a small, house-shaped casket made of ivory plates bound with brass strips and decorated with delicately carved medallions.

In the ninth or tenth century, the monks of Padstow annotated a copy of the gospels from Brittany, which is the only surviving manuscript from a Cornish monastery. On its spare leaves and in its margins the monks recorded the liberation of slaves; most of the slaves were Cornish, while most of their owners were Saxon. The Padstow community brought the book to Bodmin when they fled the Viking raids; it is known as the *Bodmin Gospels* and is now in the British Museum. The monastery at Bodmin flourished during the Saxon period and its monks spread throughout the south-west. The impressive church contains an elaborately decorated late Norman font, dating from the twelfth century. At least eight Cornish chapels and wells are dedicated to Petroc, and he was even more popular beyond Cornwall; there are a number of churches dedicated to him in Wales.

# Piran

The earliest reference to Piran is the place name Carnperan (or 'Rock of Piran'), recorded at Perranzabuloe in 960. Piran's surviving *Life* was probably written in the twelfth or thirteenth century in Cornwall or at Exeter cathedral. It is an adaptation of the *Life* of the Irish monk Ciarán of Saighir, but Piran is more likely to have been Cornish than Irish. By 1086 a minster church with a large parish was dedicated to him at Perranzabuloe (meaning 'Piran in the sands'). Piran later became the patron saint of tin miners, who worked in the area. There are a number of other dedications to Piran on the north Cornish coast, and more on the south coast near the pilgrim routes to and from Brittany.

One of Cornwall's chief medieval shrines was that of Piran at Perranporth, 7 miles north-west of Truro. All that remains today is a fine Celtic cross beside a ruined medieval church. The outline of the churchyard, still partly visible in the sand dunes, probably delineates the boundary wall of the Celtic monastery, which was called Lanpiran; the wall enclosed both the cross and the church. Four hundred metres to the west is the site of a pre-Norman chapel, buried beneath the sand; the site is marked by a tall wooden cross. This was Piran's shrine, which has been excavated several times and was last buried in 1981. Its walls are of unhewn, cemented stones, leaning inwards to minimise roof stress. The chapel's east wall perhaps dates from Piran's time.

*Celtic cross, Perranporth.*

Before the dunes encroached, Piran's oratory stood at the head of a small valley. Pilgrims drank from a spring that rose beside the chapel and flowed down to the sea. In the eleventh or twelfth century, a north door was constructed to ease the flow of pilgrims, so that they could pass through the chapel to venerate Piran's relics, and leave by the door on the opposite side. A thirteenth-century document describes a reliquary containing Piran's skull, which was placed in a niche above the altar, and a shrine containing his body, which rested on the chancel floor. Piran's small copper bell and his pectoral cross carved out of bone were also preserved, together with his pastoral staff, which was decorated with gold, silver and precious stones. These disappeared in the seventeenth century.

Pirran's shrine was overwhelmed by the sand in medieval times. In the seventeenth century, mining caused the Penwortha stream to go underground. Drifting sand does not cross running water, and until this time the Penwortha had protected the parish church from the encroaching dunes, but with the disappearance of the stream, the parish church too was gradually engulfed in sand; it was abandoned in 1804. To find the site, take the B3285 from Goonhavern in the direction of Perranporth. The 'lost church' is signed to the right, at a sharp bend in the road. Turn right here and park in a layby opposite the first road to the right. Take the footpath left across Penhale Sands, then bear right, following some of the many white marker posts. After 15 minutes, look for a Celtic cross or ask a fellow walker. The ruined church is visible in the sand beyond the cross.

## Sadwrn

Sadwrn is Welsh for Saturninus. This saint was educated in the Romano-British church of south Wales and was said to be a brother of Illtud. In medieval times he was known as *Farchog* (or 'the Knight'), and was said to have married a kinswoman, a Breton princess named Canna. They ended their days on Anglesey, where Sadwrn founded a church at Llansadwrn, 3 miles west of Beaumaris. His tombstone, dating from about 530, is set in the chancel wall.

*Sadwrn's tombstone, Llansadwrn, Anglesey.*

It is written in Latin and was carved in Roman capitals by his immediate followers. It reads: HIC BEATUS SATURNINUS SEPULTUS IACIT ET SUA SANCTA CONIUX. PAX [VOBISCUM SIT], or 'Here lies blessed Saturninus and his saintly wife. Peace be with you both.'

Winifred's twelfth-century *Life* relates that after leaving Holywell, she moved inland with her nuns to Bodfari, and then continued south-west for 7 miles until she reached the church of Sadwrn at Henllan. Later, the church may have fallen into ruin, for Henllan means 'old, or former, church'. The large fourteenth-century church that can be seen today is built on sloping ground above a stream, on the site of a smaller, earlier church, from which the font and a single pillar have been preserved; they are in the churchyard near the porch. The embattled fourteenth-century tower stands on a rock, south-east of the church; this was probably to avoid adding its considerable weight to the church, which may have been considered to be on insecure ground, on the hillside. The tower retains its original oak door.

## Samson

We know a considerable amount about Samson (c. 490–c. 565), because a long and interesting *Life of Samson* survives; it was written by a Breton monk, perhaps as early as the seventh century. Samson was born of a wealthy family in south-west Wales. His parents took him to St Illtud's famous school at Llanilltud Fawr, in the Vale of Glamorgan, where Samson later became a monk. Samson was ordained a priest and went to the monastery's daughter house on Caldey Island off the Pembrokeshire coast; in time he became its abbot. He later visited Ireland, where he acquired a chariot or light cart in which to travel. He put the cart on a boat and returned to Llanilltud Fawr, where he was invited to become abbot; he was consecrated a bishop in about 521. With his father Amon and two companions, Samson then withdrew to a quieter place, a ruined fort near the Welsh bank of the River Severn.

Samson next decided to travel as a pilgrim for Christ. He sailed to Cornwall with a group of relatives, landing at Padstow and continuing up the Camel estuary until they came within 2 miles of the monastery of Docco, now named St Kew. They hoped to stay here, but the community sent one of their number, Juvanius, to dissuade Samson from doing so, since the community had grown lax. The group continued southwards across Cornwall. As they travelled, they met a group of people with their chieftain, 'celebrating the mysteries of their ancestors'. Samson carved a cross on a standing stone and healed a boy who had fallen unconscious from his horse. The ruler told his followers to come forward and reaffirm their baptism. He next asked Samson to drive an evil serpent from a cave, which the monk did. According to tradition, the cave can still be seen at Golant, 2 miles north of Fowey, where a church and holy well are named after Samson.

We read in Samson's *Life* that after he had killed the serpent, the grateful chief and his followers asked Samson to become their bishop. He refused, but accepted the offer of the cave as a retreat. Samson's cave can be seen at Golant, down by the harbour. It is beside the railway, behind the third telegraph pole alongside the track. It is a long cavern and can be explored only with wellingtons and a torch. Samson's biographer has an explanation for the water which floods the cave: 'One day he was thirsty ... After he had prayed, he saw water dripping in a continuous shower from the rocky roof of the cave ... and to this day that water does not cease flowing, day or night.'

Golant church is high above the harbour and the cave. It contains a fine wooden pulpit dating from the fifteenth century. One of its panels depicts Samson as a bishop; this may once have formed part of the rood screen. He is a solid figure whose furrowed brow reflects the cares of his office. He stands with dignity, his head framed in a recess which also forms his halo. At the west end of the church, a modern stained glass window depicts scenes from Samson's

*Samson's holy well, Golant church, Cornwall.*

life, including his encounter with the 'poisonous and most evil serpent'. Beside the church porch is Samson's holy well in a medieval well house.

Half a mile to the west is Castle Dore hill fort, where the chieftain and his followers may have lived. It was defended by two well-preserved circular ramparts; inside, there were many roundhouses. The fortress can best be approached from the B3269, by walking along the track to Lawhibbet Farm. The fort is in the first field to the right. Paul Aurelian, another early monk, is described as visiting a ruler named Mark and styled Cunomorus (or 'Sea Dog'), probably at Castle Dore. Cunomorus is named on a sixth-century pillar stone which was found nearby; it can be seen beside the road as it leads into Fowey, in a layby on the left. The son of Cunomorus was named Drustan. The two men may have become King Mark and his nephew Tristan in the later legend of King Arthur.

Samson established a monastery, perhaps at Fowey, leaving his father Amon in charge of the new community; he then sailed to Brittany with his followers. He founded Dol, on the north coast, and several other monasteries. He signed decrees of Church Councils in Paris in 553 and 557. On one of his journeys to Paris, a wheel fell off his much-used chariot. Samson took an active part in Breton politics, and has dedications in eastern Brittany and Normandy. A town in Guernsey and one of the Scilly Isles are named after him.

# Seiriol

A local Anglesey saint, Seiriol is honoured at Penmon near the north-eastern tip of Anglesey, 3 miles north-north-east of Beaumaris. The monastery at Penmon was said to have been founded by Einion, Prince of Lleyn, who appointed his nephew, Seiriol, as head of the community. As with many early Christian sites, the isolation of its idyllic setting is misleading, for the monastery is surrounded by four clusters of hut circles, the remains of a large Celtic village of at least 300 inhabitants. Between the groups of homes, terraces survive to show that farming was practised. The circular stone wall of Seiriol's hut rests snugly against a sheltering cliff. Beside its remains are the foundations of his well and its antechamber, where several people could sit. The brickwork over the well dates from the eighteenth century; the red bricks do not blend with the solid stones that surround the pool below. The well was revered through the centuries, and the well keeper lived in a house nearby until relatively recently.

The present church was built in the twelfth century to replace a wooden one burnt by the Danes in 971. Two fine tenth-century carved crosses are preserved inside the church. They show both Irish and Scandinavian influence, and are thought to originate from a school of sculptors based in Cheshire. From the monastery there is a magnificent view across the Conwy Bay towards the mountains on the mainland, where Seiriol was said to have a hermitage at Penmaenmawr.

Another group of monks lived on Ynys Seiriol (now Puffin Island), half a mile offshore. The monastic cemetery was also on the island, and many monks and rulers were buried here, including Seiriol and his cousin, Maelgwyn, King of Gwynedd. The island was not always a safe haven: in 632 King Cadwallon took refuge there while

*Seiriol's circular hut and well house, Penmon, Anglesey.*

King Edwin of Northumbria laid siege to the tiny island, before capturing Anglesey. Norse settlers named the island 'Priestholm' after the priests who lived there. In medieval times, Seiriol's body was brought back from Priestholm to Penmon, and buried in a shrine in the church crypt, beneath the chancel; pilgrims descended a stone staircase to visit it.

Writing in the twelfth century, Gerald of Wales informs us that Penmon was one of three reformed Culdee monasteries in north Wales. This was a movement which originated in Ireland in the ninth century. Groups of monks who called themselves *Céli Dé* (or 'Servants of God') encouraged a return to solitude and the rigorous ideals followed by monks of earlier times. If Penmon became a Culdee community, this suggests Irish influence, and a strong commitment to religious life. The community on Priestholm must also have flourished, for in 1237 King Lliwelyn the Great granted the monastery of Penmon to the prior of Priestholm.

Later in the century, Penmon became an Augustinian friary. Dominating the site today is the friars' thirteenth-century refectory, with a dormitory above and cellars below. The men ate in silence while one of them read aloud. There is a corner seat beside a window, where the reader could take advantage of the natural light. The friars' main source of protein was fish and their fishpond survives, fed from Seiriol's well. The Augustinians were responsible for a fine stained-glass window above Seiriol's shrine in the church. Only two fragments of the great east window remain, depicting saints Christopher and Seiriol; they are now combined in a small window in the south transept. Seiriol is dressed as a medieval friar in brown and white robes, with a cap and a curly beard.

At Clorach, a mile east of Llanerchymedd, nearer the centre of Anglesey, twin wells on either side of the road were named after Seiriol and Cybi, who, according to tradition, used to meet here. For both men, the journey was about 10 miles each way. Since Cybi faced the sun in the morning and again in the evening, he was nicknamed 'the Tanned' while Seiriol was nicknamed 'the Pale'. The wells were visited for healing as late as the nineteenth century.

# Selevan

Selevan's name comes from that of King Solomon; the Irish surname Sullivan is another form of Solomon. Celtic Christians liked to have biblical characters as their patrons: Samson, Daniel, David and Asaph, for example. Stories recorded at St Levan in the eighteenth century describe Selevan as a hermit and fisherman; he was possibly the son of a Cornish chieftain named Gereint. The hamlet of St Levan is 3 miles south-east of Land's End, where it overlooks the sea, which turns turquoise and azure as it pounds the white shingle of Chapel Cove. The church is set in a sheltered hollow above the cliffs; it is built beside a large fissured rock in the churchyard which was probably a pre-Christian holy stone. Perhaps to counteract its power, six tall, elegant crosses were erected, three at either door of the church. One still stands, almost 3m tall, and the heads of two others can be seen in the churchyard. The church contains fine medieval bench ends, with lively representations of a shepherd, a jester and a pilgrim who has visited Compostella and wears a cockle shell in his hat as a token from the Spanish shrine.

Across the road, a track leads down to Selevan's ancient baptistery, above the cove. This is a small building, 1.5m by 2.1m, constructed of giant granite slabs; it was roofed until the eighteenth century. Adjoining it is Selevan's holy well, which was known for curing eye diseases and toothache. People bathed in the well and then slept on the stone floor of the baptistery. Further down the path to the cove, a hermit's two-roomed cell can be seen, also edged with granite boulders. Excavation carried out in 1931 revealed a roughly flagged stone floor. It was built on an east-west axis, so one room may have been a chapel. This was a sheltered spot for a hermit, with easy fishing in the cove below.

*Selevan's baptistery, Chapel Cove.*

# Serf

Serf was a native missionary who is said to have worked among the southern Picts in the district around Stirling; his mother may have been a local princess. It is not known whether Serf lived in the fifth or in the eighth century, or whether there were two men with the same name working in this area. The 'early' Serf was said to have been ordained by Palladius, a deacon from Auxerre who accompanied Germanus on a mission to Ireland in 431 to combat the Pelagian heresy. Serf's cult centre was at Culross, on the northern shore of the Firth of Forth, 12 miles south-east of Stirling. There are other churches dedicated to him in the region at Dunning, Alva, Tillicoultry and Clackmannan. An island in Loch Leven, 7 miles west of Glenrothes, is perhaps dedicated to the eighth-century Serf.

The twelfth-century monk, Jocelyn of Furness, relates that the young Kentigern trained at a monastery in Culross, under its abbot, Serf. Culross is a picturesque town with its cobbled streets and sixteenth-century merchants' houses with their gabled roofs. The site of Serf's monastery can be found on the hill above the town. Under the ruins of a thirteenth-century Cistercian abbey are traces of an early Christian church, with its altar beneath the present one. A reliquary set inside a niche in the ruined south wall of the nave once contained Serf's bones.

A few streets below, a deep well in Erskine Brae was the monastery's source of water; it was covered over in the nineteenth century. Coal is plentiful on both sides of the Firth of Forth, and the monks of Culross became the region's first coalminers. Culross owes its prosperity to this discovery: the coal lay near the surface and was easily transported by sea. The abbey was established for the Cistercians by Malcolm, Earl of Fife, in 1217. Beside the road leading into Culross are the ruins of a chapel

*View from Culross monastery over the Firth of Forth.*

built by Archbishop Blackadder of Glasgow in 1503 in honour of Kentigern's birth. The twelfth-century *Life of Kentigern* relates that his disgraced mother floated ashore here and gave birth to her son. Only the chapel's walls and its altar survive.

According to his medieval *Life*, Serf's earliest and favourite Christian settlement was at Dunning, on the old road from Perth to Stirling, 8 miles south-west of Perth. There was an ancient village at Dunning, where six roads meet. Serf is said to have slain a dragon here with his staff; part of the village is named Dray-gon. The story may describe how Serf released the people from the grip of paganism, through the authority of his pastoral staff. Dunning's church has a late Celtic doorway, perhaps dating from the tenth century, and a steeple built in about 1170. Housed in the church is a magnificent early ninth-century cross, which was carved to honour Constantine, who was King of the Picts from about 789 to 820.

Serf is also honoured at Dysart, now a north-eastern suburb of Kirkcaldy, in Fife; it is situated on the northern shore of the Firth of Forth as it broadens, east of Edinburgh. The name Dysart comes from the Latin word *desertum*, which means an empty place; Serf is said to have lived alone here in a cave beside the shore. It can be found in the grounds of a Carmelite convent, where the cave's roof is visible over the convent wall. Across the road is the fortified tower of Serf's medieval church.

# Sidwell

The biographer of Paul Aurelian tells us that Paul had a sister named Sitofolla, a nun who lived near the seashore. She may be the saint named Sidwell whose relics were honoured in a church outside the east gate of Exeter by 1135, close to a well which bore her name. People came to her shrine for healing throughout medieval times. In the twelfth century, the bishop of Exeter compiled a book of liturgical readings for use in the cathedral, which records Sidwell's story as it was then told: her stepmother had her murdered by labourers reaping in the fields, who cut off her head with their scythes. This preserves a pre-Christian myth in which the harvest goddess was said to die when reapers cut the last sheaf of corn. Sidwell is depicted with her scythe on rood screens, bench ends and windows in about 20 churches.

The Cornish church of Laneast on the edge of Bodmin Moor is dedicated

*St Sidwell's holy well, Laneast.*

to Sidwell. Six miles west of Launceston, Laneast is a quiet hamlet on the north-eastern edge of Bodmin Moor, above the River Inney. A Celtic cross stands outside the church porch, which has fine carved medieval roof beams. Elaborate porch roofs are a feature of a number of churches in this area. There is a Norman font decorated with wheel crosses and carvings of four human heads, and medieval carved bench ends, including a fine representation of a green man.

To find the well, walk out of the churchyard and continue for 100m east-south-east along the road to the triangle of waste ground beside the farm. To the right of the white house opposite the farm, a signed track leads into a field and down to the well, which is about 300m from the road. It is housed in a fine granite-roofed building, perhaps dating from the sixteenth century. Its water flows downhill to join the River Inney. It was formerly used for christenings and is also called Jordan Well, to recall the baptism of Jesus. For the same reason, church fonts were sometimes called Jordans.

## Sulien

Said to be a follower of the Breton monk Cadfan, Sulien has dedications in Brittany and two churches in Cornwall at Tresilian and Luxulyan. Luxulyan (*loc*, or 'place' of Sulien) is the only Cornish example of the prefix *loc*, a common feature in Breton place names, which suggests that Luxulyan church may have been a Breton foundation. Luxulyan is in moorland 4 miles north-east of St Austell, in mid Cornwall. Its church was built over what was probably a large pre-Christian burial mound. A Cornish cross is set in the wall outside the west door. Inside the church is a fine late Norman twelfth-century font with monsters and a tree of life carved around its bowl. The heads of the four evangelists are carved on supporting pillars at each corner.

The ancient church of Corwen in mid Wales is also dedicated to Mael and Sulien; it is at the foot of the Berwyn Mountains, beside the fast-flowing River Dee, and the town grew alongside an important route for travellers through the centuries. This was the Roman road along which Welsh drovers also herded their cattle, later becoming the A5, the main road from London to Holyhead. The name Corwen means 'stone church' (or, literally, 'choir-white'). This is a Welsh version of the English name Whitchurch, and denotes an important

*Cross on a Bronze Age boulder with cup marks, Corwen churchyard.*

stone church, at a time when others were more simply constructed of timber.

Corwen church is built on an ancient holy site, beside a prehistoric standing stone, named in Welsh 'The pointed stone in the icy corner'. When the building was enlarged in medieval times, the ancient stone was incorporated into the wall of the porch. In the churchyard is a large Bronze Age boulder with seven cup marks, which might be holes into which libations could be poured. The boulder was 'Christianised' some time between the ninth and the twelfth centuries and used as the base for a tall cross. A well in Cwm parish on the slopes of the Clwyd range is also named after the two monks; its water cured eye diseases.

# Teilo

Teilo was a sixth-century monk and bishop, whose cult was centred on Llandeilo Fawr, above the River Tywi in south Wales. He may have been born in Penally, on the coast near Tenby. In about 1130 Geoffrey of Llandaff wrote a biographical sermon about Teilo, in which he relates that he was a pupil of Dubricius and Paul Aurelian. During the plague, he went to Brittany for seven years, staying with Samson at Dol. We are told that he then returned to Wales and died in Llandeilo Fawr.

The extent of the Celtic monastery is outlined by the very large churchyard of 3½ acres. It is bisected by the town's main street, which may follow the line of a Roman road. A spring rises near the east end of the church and flows into a large chamber beneath it. This may be the site of a baptistery in which converts were immersed. The spring provided the town with its water until the nineteenth century; today it bubbles into an alcove on the outside of the churchyard wall.

Teilo was buried at Llandeilo Fawr. His cult became popular in south Wales, where 33 churches are named after him. Remains of two finely carved crosses from the late eighth century show the continuing importance of the community; that in the photo draws upon elements from prehistoric cup and ring marks and contemporary embossed metalwork.

A magnificent Irish or Mercian gospel book, illuminated in about 730, was given to the monastery around 820 'for the good of his soul' by a man named Gelhi, who had bought the book from a certain Guyal in exchange for his best horse. The gospel book contains stylised figures of the four evangelists: Luke holds a pastoral staff modelled on those carried by abbots of the Near East, and there are whole pages of intricate eastern-style 'carpet' decoration in which fish, dogs and pelicans are intertwined.

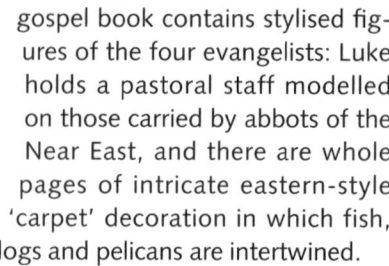

*Llandeilo Fawr: eighth-century cross head.*

## Trillo

A disciple of Cadfan, Trillo was said to have been a priest on Bardsey Island. The tiny medieval chapel of Llandrillo-yn-Rhos ('church of Trillo on the promontory'), a mile north-west of Colwyn Bay, is named after him. The chapel is situated improbably below the Victorian promenade, close to the shore. Inside the tiny thirteenth-century building, in front of the altar, is a rectangular pool. This encloses the freshwater spring which Trillo or his unknown follower used for drinking, bathing and baptising converts. Beside the chapel are the remains of his circular hut. Further up the hill from the beach, the parish church is also dedicated to Trillo.

Trillo is also honoured in the village of Llandrillo, 30 miles inland over the moors, on a tributary of the River Dee, where his medieval church stands beside an ancient yew tree. Across the river, at the foot of an oak, is Trillo's holy well, which cured rheumatism; it flowed until 100 years ago. Two stories about the well illustrate how saints were believed to punish those who did not treat their wells with reverence. This spring was originally in the corner of a low-lying field, but in about 1855 the tenant farmer objected to 'trespassers' visiting the well. It therefore ran dry, and reappeared in a neighbouring farmer's field! In another story, the well dried up because someone threw a dead cat or dog into it. By 1913, the spring no longer flowed, except in winter or after heavy rain.

*Chapel built over Trillo's holy well, Llandrillo-yn-Rhos.*

## Tudno

Little is known about Tudno, to whom a church is dedicated on the headland of the Great Orme, above the modern town of Llandudno (or 'church site of Tudno'), 3 miles north-west of Colwyn Bay in north Wales. A limestone cave containing a freshwater spring on the shore below the church is named after Tudno, and there is another ancient well near his church. Tudno attracted bardic legend: one of the 13 treasures of Britain was said to be Tudno's whetstone, which sharpened the sword of a hero but blunted that of a coward.

A stone church was built here in the twelfth century and the carved bowl of its font still survives. In medieval times, Llandudno was still a cluster of farms around Tudno's church, and it remained a small community until a holiday resort grew along the strand below in the nineteenth century. The key of the church is held at the farm below the churchyard. To find Tudno's well, walk up the road past the church and take the second footpath to the left towards Pink Farm, signed 'Ski Llandudno'. The well is on the right, 100 yards along the track, just inside a field.

The Great Orme (a name derived from the Old Norse for 'great worm', or sea serpent) was well known in early times – copper was mined here from the Bronze Age until the nineteenth century. A flock of feral goats has been reintroduced onto the Great Orme; they roamed wild in Celtic times and feature in the lives of the monks. However, the goats which one sees here today are from Kashmir and have lived on the Orme since the 1890s.

*Feral goats, Llandudno.*

# Tysilio

A younger son of Brochwel, King of Powys, Tysilio's name means 'dear Sunday's child', so he was probably born on a Sunday. He lived in the early seventh century and according to his late *Life*, he studied under a hermit named Gwyddfarch at the monastery of Meifod in central Wales, 5 miles north-west of Welshpool. A number of churches dedicated to Tysilio are situated close to royal forts of Brochwel's household. Two more settlements are named after him in south Wales, with another to the south-east in the Wye valley. Tysilio's *Life* was written by a Breton monk in the fifteenth century, but it is unreliable and may be a conflation of stories about two different men.

At Meifod, the churchyard of 9 acres may indicate the extent of the Celtic monastery, which in time contained three churches, one named after its founder, Gwyddfarch (its remains were still visible in the seventeenth century); one named after Tysilio; and a third which was a pre-Norman dedication to Our Lady. The monastery became the mother church of Powys and the burial place of its kings – a fine Celtic tombstone in the church may mark a royal burial. It represents the triumph of God over evil, and is bordered by serpents and asymmetrical interlacing patterns. In the centre is a Latin cross and above it is a Greek crucifix, on which hangs Jesus with pierced hands.

Tysilio's *Life* relates that he later returned to Meifod and became abbot in place of the now elderly Gwyddfarch. When Gwyddfarch died, he was buried outside the village, at the top of Allt-y-Ancr ('anchorite's hill'). Tysilio rebuilt the monastery church and the twelfth-century poet Cynddelw described this achievement:

> He raised a church with fostering hand;
> a church with bright lights,
> and a chancel for offerings,
> a church above the stream, by the glassy waters,
> a church of Powys, paradise most fair.

The present Norman church was built in 1154 by Madoc ap Meredydd, Prince of Powys, the last ruler under whom Powys experienced political unity and independence. The Norman arches are constructed of red sandstone which was little used in the area, and was probably expensive and difficult to obtain. Prince Madoc also rebuilt the shrine of St Melangell at Pennant Melangell, using the same school of craftsmen.

At some point in his life, Tysilio is said to have become a hermit on a tiny island named after him in the Menai Strait. It can be visited by walking down through the woods, a little beyond the Anglesey end of the Menai Bridge. There is a small car park at the approach to the woods. On the island, a single-chambered church dating from the fifteenth century probably stands on the site of a Celtic chapel. Many dead are buried around Tysilio's church. The islet is reached by a causeway, from which one can watch curlews, oystercatchers and a colony of terns. In spring, the island is golden with primroses. Behind the church are the Swellies: dangerous tidal currents.

*St Tysilio's church, Llandysilio Island.*

An eighteenth-century traveller, Thomas Pennard, described how 'as a very young man, I ventured myself in a small boat into the midst of the boiling waves and mill-race current'. The next settlement along the coast is Llanfairpwllgwyngyll, whose full name describes both the Swellies and Tysilio's tiny church. When translated it reads: 'Church of St Mary by the pool with the white hazels, near the fierce whirlpool by the church of St Tysilio, near the red cave'. In spite of continuous traffic over the Menai Bridge, Llandysilio Island has retained its peaceful atmosphere through the centuries.

# Winifred

The name Winifred means 'radiant Freda' (*gwen Frewi* in Welsh) and in north Wales, her cult is ancient and widespread. When her relics were taken to Shrewsbury abbey in 1138, its monks wrote the *Legend of St Winifred*. She is described as a princess who was beheaded by Caradoc, the son of a neighbouring prince, whom she had refused to marry. A spring flowed at Holywell where her head fell to the ground, but her uncle, St Beuno, raised her to life. The legend is one of many in which a saint is decapitated and a healing spring flows where their blood touches the earth.

According to the *Legend of St Winifred*, she established a convent of nuns at Holywell, which is near the Flintshire coast, 15 miles north-west of Chester. Here, Winifred's well was known for its healing properties and has attracted pilgrims throughout the centuries. In the fifteenth century, King Henry V walked the 50 miles from Shrewsbury to Holywell. When King Edward IV made a similar pilgrimage in 1480, Tudur Aled wrote: 'Garlands on garlands decked the way; thousands trampled down the greensward.' He noted how the king reverently sprinkled soil from the shrine on his crown. Lady Margaret Beaufort, King Henry VII's mother, built the present chapel with its star-shaped pool in 1483, to replace an earlier Norman chapel. A carving on a corner roof corbel shows a pilgrim carrying an invalid on his back; the sick are still carried through the bathing pool in this way.

Jesuits and other priests lived at Holywell throughout penal times, when Catholics could be fined or imprisoned for worshipping openly. The well became a centre of resistance to the 'new religion' of Protestantism. Daniel Defoe wrote that priests were 'very numerous' here, but had to appear in disguise. In May 1719, hearing that Catholics intended to celebrate St Winifred's day, the authorities sent in dragoons who seized the priest during the Eucharist, together with the church plate and richly decorated statues. In 1722 the church was confiscated and became a day school; 'however, to supply the loss of this chapel, the Roman Catholics have chapels erected in almost every inn, for the devotion of the pilgrims that flock thither from all the popish parts of England'.

In the eighteenth century, Lancashire pilgrims visiting Holywell crossed the Mersey by boat, walked across the Wirral and the often treacherous sands of the Dee estuary at low tide, and climbed the narrow valley to Winifred's well. The ancient landing stage at Holywell can still be seen; here, local fishermen bring in their catch. The pilgrims travelled in groups and lit beacons on the Wirral to signal for a boat on their way home. In 1795 Thomas Pennard visited the shrine and wrote: 'In the summer, still a few are to be seen in the water in deep devotion up to their chins for hours, sending up their prayers.'

In the following century, opposition to visiting the well waned, and the town council became aware of its possibilities. A hospice for pilgrims was opened in 1870 and at a meeting of the town council in 1896 the chairman stated: 'In the past year, 1,710 pilgrims, many sick and pitifully afflicted, were housed at the hospice ... Of these, upwards of 500 were examined and registered by the medical attendant, and I am assured by him that a great many remarkable cures were obtained.' To this day, many continue to come to the shrine for healing.

*Star-shaped pool, Holywell.*

Winifred's *Legend* relates that her uncle, Beuno, came to Holywell, where he obtained land from her parents on which to build a church. This may have been on the site of the fifteenth-century parish church, on the hillside above Winifred's well. Across the road, on top of Castle Hill, Beuno's well is almost inaccessible beneath undergrowth. It flows into a stream on the embankment which surrounds the hill fort, where it is possible that Winifred's family may have lived.

According to her *Legend*, Winifred later travelled inland with a group of nuns, until she reached the remote settlement of Gwytherin. The hamlet is 12 miles south of Colwyn Bay, in the valley of the River Cledwen. As one drives towards it, Snowdon's peak is often visible across the Vale of Conwy. A monk named Eleri was said to have founded a monastery at Gwytherin; his mother, Theonia, was its first leader. Gwytherin was already a holy place: above a burial mound, two yew trees, now over 2000 years old were planted on an east-west axis, aligned with the rising and setting sun. Between them is a row of four pre-Christian standing stones. In the fifth or sixth century, one of these was reused as a tombstone by a Christian family, for inscribed on it in Latin is '[The stone of] Vinnemaglus, son of Senemaglus'.

According to her *Legend*, Winifred succeeded Theonia as abbess, and died here; in about the eighth century her bones were enshrined in a house-shaped wooden reliquary, decorated with ornamental metalwork. Gwytherin's single-chambered church was rebuilt in the nineteenth century. A late Celtic grave slab inscribed with a cross is set in the chancel step, and nearby is a medieval chest, carved from a single tree trunk, for offerings at Winifred's shrine. There was a flourishing monastery here in medieval times, a double community for both monks and nuns. A survey of 1334 mentions abbots at Gwytherin. The churchyard was larger than it is today; it included Winifred's *capel y bedd*, or chapel of her grave. In the seventeenth century, the antiquarian Edward Lhuyd wrote that it was still standing; it was demolished early in the following century. Lhuyd sketched her casket shrine in about 1696, calling it 'St Winifred's Chest', but it has now disappeared.

## Winwaloe: see Guénolé

# MAPS

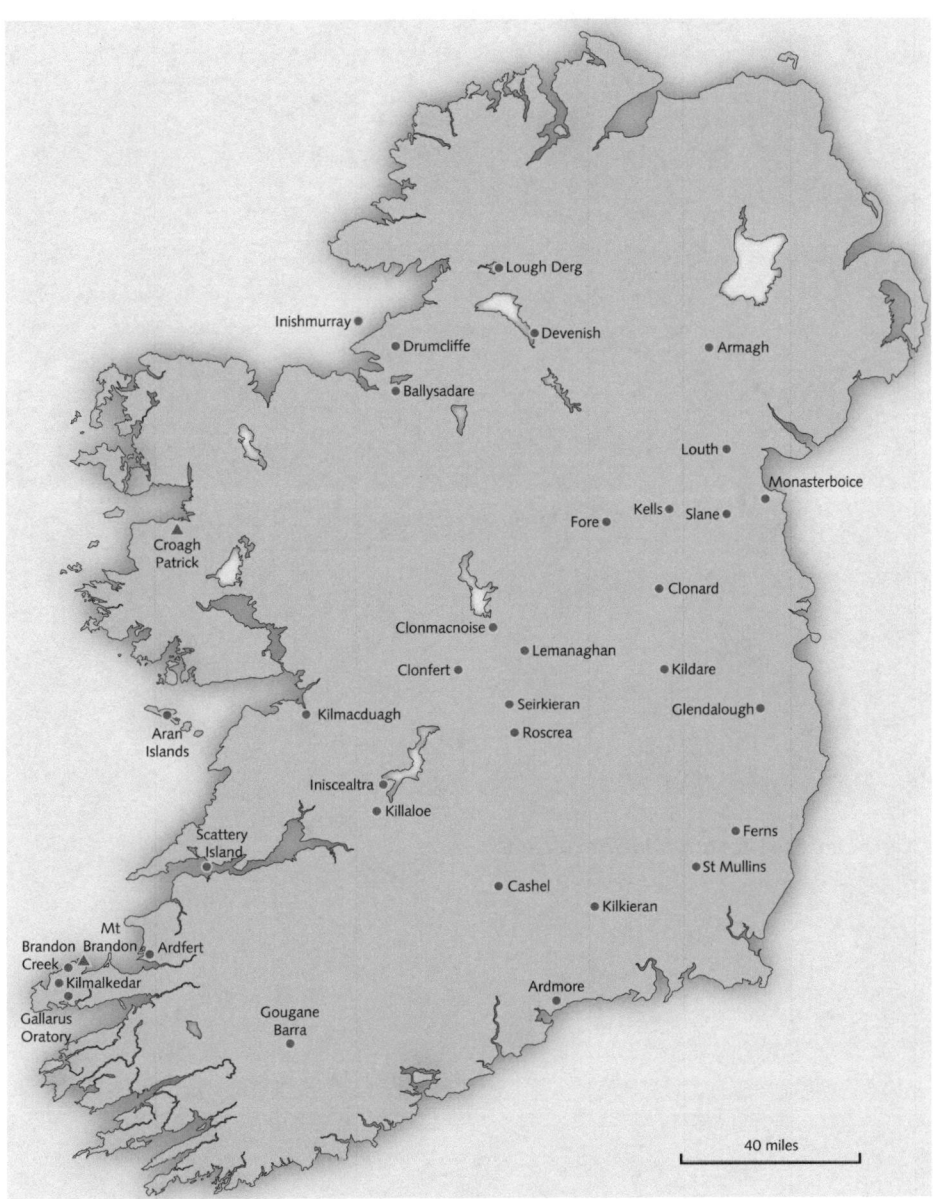

Early Christian sites of Ireland

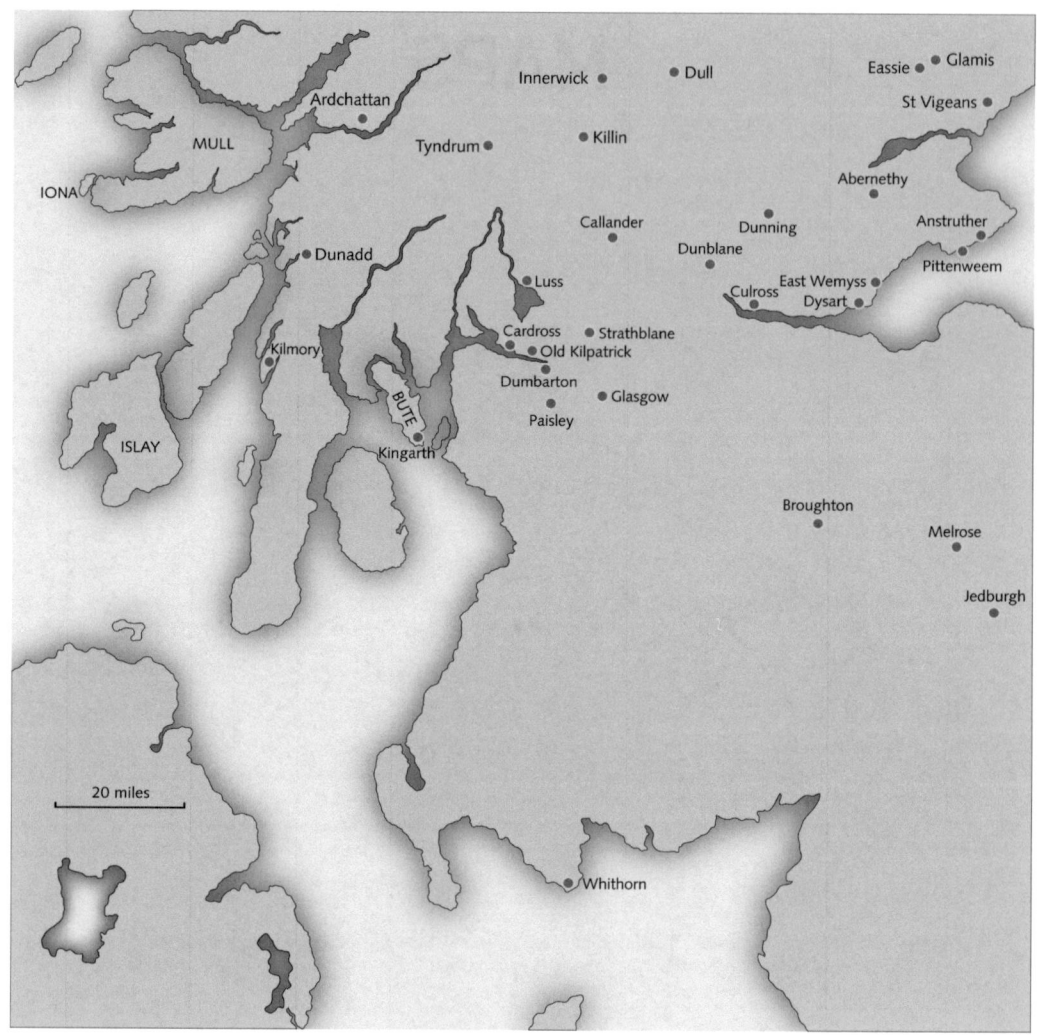

*Early Christian sites of Southern Scotland*

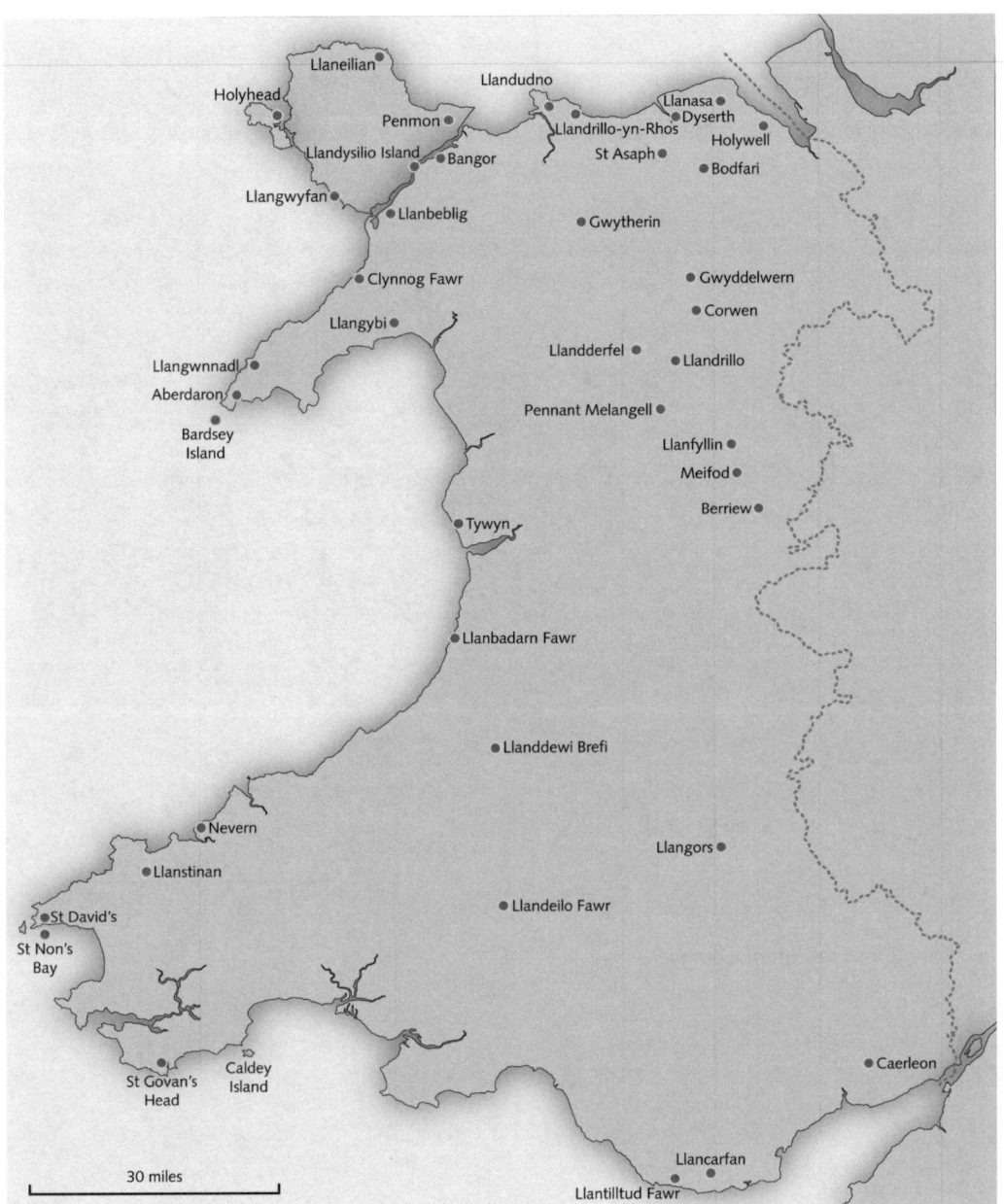

*Early Christian sites of Wales*

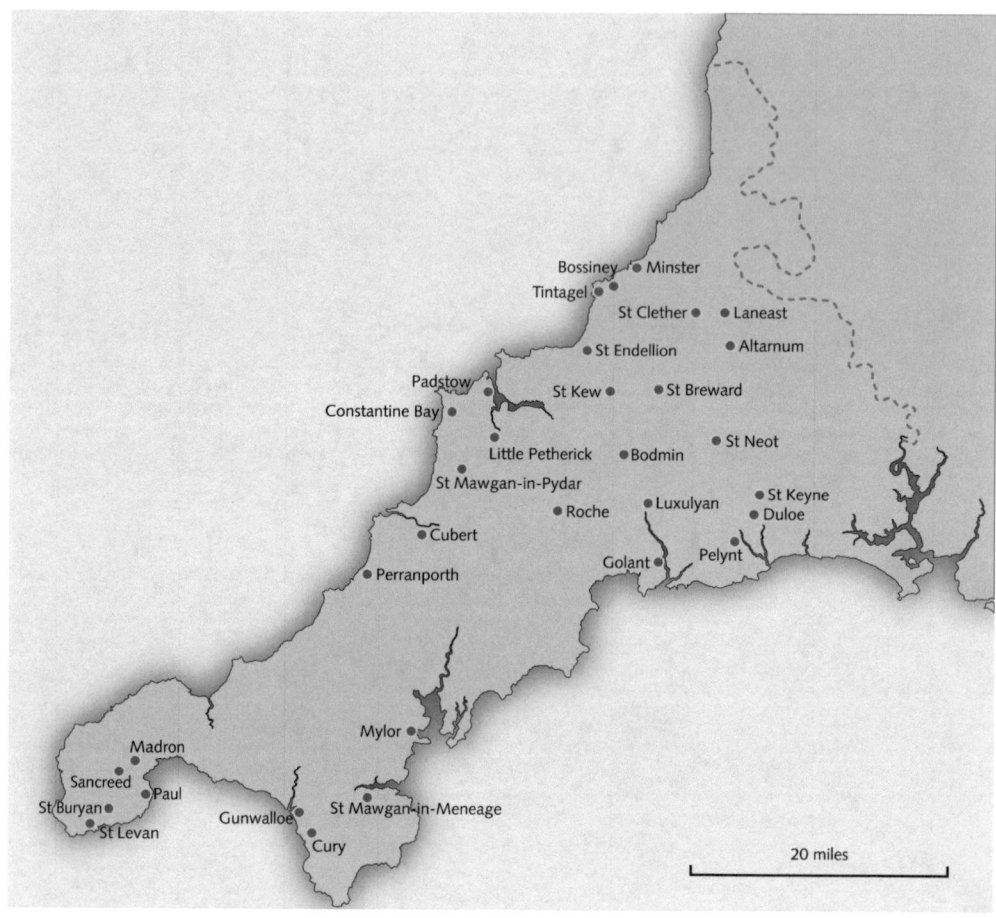

*Early Christian sites of Cornwall*

# FURTHER READING

Bragg, M., *Credo* (London, Sceptre, 1996)

Carmichael, A., *Carmina Gadelica* (Edinburgh, Floris, 1994)

Cartwright, J., ed., *Celtic Hagiography and Saints' Cults* (Cardiff, University of Wales Press, 2003)

Costen, M. *The Origins of Somerset* (Manchester, Manchester University Press, 1992)

Davies, O., *Celtic Christianity in Early Medieval Wales: The Origins of the Welsh Spiritual Tradition* (Cardiff, University of Wales Press, 1996)

Davies, O., *Celtic Spirituality*, 'Classics of Western Spirituality' Series (New Jersey, Paulist Press, 1999)

Guest, C., *The Mabinogion* (New York, Dover Publications, 1997)

Hill, P., *Whithorn and St Ninian: the Excavation of a Monastic Town 1984–91* (Stroud, Sutton Publishing, 1997)

Jones, F., *The Holy Wells of Wales* (Cardiff, University of Wales Press, 1992)

Low, M., *Celtic Christianity and Nature* (Belfast, Black Star Press, 1996)

Manning, C., *Early Irish Monasteries* (Dublin, Town House & Country House, 1995)

Manning, C., *Clonmacnoise* (Dublin, Dúchas, 1998)

Marsden, J., *The Illustrated Columcille* (London, Macmillan, 1991)

Meyrick, J., *A Pilgrim's Guide to the Holy Wells of Cornwall* (Falmouth, Meyrick, 1982)

O'Loughlin, T., *St Patrick: The Man and His Works* (London, SPCK, 1999)

O'Loughlin, T., *Journeys on the Edges: The Celtic Tradition* (London, Darton, Longman and Todd, 2000)

Orme, N., *The Saints of Cornwall* (Oxford, Oxford University Press, 2000)

Petts, D., *Christianity in Roman Britain* (Stroud, Tempus, 2003)

Rees, E., *Celtic Saints of Wessex* (Salisbury, Wessex Books, 2007)

Rees, E., *Celtic Saints in their Landscape*, 2nd ed. (Stroud, Amberley Publishing, 2011)

Richter, M., *Medieval Ireland – The Enduring Tradition*, New Gill History of Ireland, vol.1 (Dublin, Gill and Macmillan, 2005)

Sharpe, R., *Medieval Irish Saints' Lives: an Introduction to* Vitae Sanctorum Hiberniae (Oxford, Oxford University Press, 1991)

Smith, D., *Celtic Travellers: Scotland in the Age of the Saints* (Edinburgh, Stationery Office, 1997)

Thomas, C., *And Shall These Mute Stones Speak?* (Cardiff, University of Wales Press, 1994)

Watson, W. J., *The History of the Celtic Place-names of Scotland* (Edinburgh, Birlinn, 1993)

Wood, M., *In Search of the Dark Ages* (London, BBC Worldwide Ltd, 2003)

# INDEX OF PLACE NAMES

Aberdaron 82, 99, 100
Aberdeen 75
Aberdeenshire 4, 13
Aberffraw 54
Abernethy 28
Aberystwyth 32, 125
Abingdon 104
Aghaboe 91-2
Alsia 32
Altarnun 123-4
Alva 139
Amesbury 118
Amlwch 70
Anglesey 19, 54, 56, 65, 70, 133-4, 135-7, 145
Angus 74
Anstruther 9
Applecross 103
Aran Islands 39, 45
Arbroath 73
Ard Oilean 73
Ardchatten 36, 37
Ardee 114
Ardfert 22, 24
Ardmore 61-3
Argyll 46, 104
Armagh 42, 102, 126
Athlone 40
Auchtertyre 76

Bala 66
Ballina 74
Ballinasloe 23
Ballysadare 74
Bamburgh 15, 16
Bandry 94
Banff 13
Bangor (Ireland) 49, 103, 112, 115
Bangor (Menai) 65, 83
Bangor-is-y-Coed 65
Bardsey Island 20, 33, 69, 82, 83, 99, 100, 143
Barmouth 32
Barnsmuir 9

Barnstaple Bay 28
Barra, Isle of 78
Barrow in Furness 12
Barry 33, 85
Bassenthwaite 12, 17, plate 23
Bath 105
Beauly 37
Beaumaris 133, 135
Belfast Lough 49, 112
Berriew 18-19
Berwick-upon-Tweed 15
Berwyn Mountains 19, 111, 141
Biggar 101
Birr 13
Black Mountains 128
Blackmore Mountains 115
Bodfari 64, 134
Bodmin 131-2
Bodmin Moor 25, 44, 119, 124, 132, 140
Boher 106
Boscastle 88, 108
Bosherston 10-11
Bossiney 118
Bradford-on-Avon 8, plate 4
Bradwell-on-Sea 38-9
Brandon Creek 23
Brandon Mountain 22
Brean 28
Brecon 28, 29, 33, 63, 128
Brefi: see Llanddewi Brefi
Breifne 42, 43
    see also: Meath
Brelade 25
Brent Knoll 28
Brest 124
Brinsea 58
Bristol 98
Bristol Channel 118
Broughton 100, 101
Brycheiniog 128-9
Bryncroes 99, 100
Burren Hills 45
Bute, Isle of 13, 20, 36-7

Cadbury Camp, Congresbury 57
Caergybi (Holyhead) 56
Caerhun 64
Caerleon 7, 33
Caernarfon 19, 83
Caerwent 33
Caiplie 9-10, plates 8, 9
Caldey Island 68-9, 134
Callander 94
Cambuskenneth 91
Camelford 25
Cannington 36
Canterbury 125
Cardiff 82
Cardigan Bay 68
Cardinham 119
Carhampton 35-6
Carlisle 92, 120
Carlow 78, 115
Carn Euny 72-3
Carnanton 124
Carn Ingli 29
Carrick-on-Suir 43
Cashel 24, 93, 107, 126
Castle Dore 128, 136
Castlepollard 73
Ceredigion 35, 53, 56, 59, 122
Chapel Cove 138
Chapel Euny 72, 73
Cheddar 49
Chedworth 8, plate 3
Cheltenham 8
Chelvey 28
Cheshire 136
Chester 64, 100, 146
Cirencester 7
Clackmannan 139
Clare, County 42, 45, 52
Clear Island 42
Clew Bay 127
Clonard 39, 78-9, 102
Clonfert 22, 23-4
Clonmacnoise 11, 39-42, 48, 79, 106, plate 22
Clorach 137
Clwyd Range 142
Clyde 36
Clyde, Firth of 36, 93, 126
Clynnog Fawr 19-20
Coldingham 16
Colwyn Bay 143, 144, 148
Cong 73
Congresbury 57-8
Connemara 73, 127
Constantine 51

Conwy 136, 148
Cork 61, 77
Cork, County 42
Cornouaille 52
Corwen 141-2
Cotswolds 57, 105
Crantock 35
Crediton 57
Croagh Patrick 127
Crosthwaite 92
Crowan 72
Crowland 119
Cubert 53
Culbone 49
Culross 92, 139
Cumbria 12, 92, plates 23, 24
Cury 52
Cwm 142

Dalriada 46, 48
Denbigh 64
Denbighshire 54, 79
Derry 46, 48, 91
Devon 28, 71, 91, 118
Dingle peninsula 11, 107, plates 20, 21
Dirinon 124
Dol 135, 142
Dolgellau 86
Donegal 13, 46, 127
Dorset 25, 102
Douglas 122
Down, County 103
Druimm-Cete 48
Drumahose 91
Drumlane 102
Dublin 23, 25, 27, 42, 53, 78, 102, 116
Duddon Sands 12
Dull 14
Duloe 55, 123
Dumbarton 126
Dumbarton Rock 126, 127
Dumfries 120
Dumnonia 51
Dunbar 17
Dunblane 20, 21
Dunboyke 102
Dundee 74, 75
Dunning 139, 140
Durrow 40, 46, 48
Dyfed 59, 63, 122
Dyrham 105
Dysart 55, 140
Dyserth 55

# INDEX OF PLACE NAMES

Eassie 75
East Weymss 9, plate 6
Edinburgh 17, 21, 77, 140
Eorpaidh 116-7
Essex 38
Exeter 31, 132, 140

Falmouth 51, 117
Farne Islands 15
Faroe Islands 23
Ferns 102-3, 115, 116
Fife 9, 73, 75, 76, 92, 139, 140, plates 6, 7, 8
Finistère 81, 84, 117, 128
Fishguard 29, 89
Fleswick Bay 18
Flintshire 19, 79
Fore 73
Forfar 13
Forth, Firth of 76, 92, 139, 140
Fowey 128, 135, 136
Furness 16, 92, 106, 139

Gallarus 8, plates 20, 21
Galloway 10, 110, 120, 121, 122
Galway 23, 45
Gartan 46
Glamis 74, 75
Glamorgan, Vale of 33, 34, 85, 134
Glasgow 92-3, 101, 112, 140
Glastonbury 11, 86, 90, 119, plate 17
Glen Dochart 76
Glen Lyon 13
Glendalough 79, 95-7, 115
Glengariff 77
Glenridding 12
Glenrothes 9, 75, 139
Gloucester 34
Gloucestershire 8, 25
Golant 117, 135
Goonhavern 133
Gorran 131
Gort 45
Gougane Barra 77
Great Orme 144
Greeba 122
Guernsey 136
Gunwalloe 81
Gwbert-on-Sea 53
Gwent 33, 68
Gwyddelwern 19
Gwynedd 65, 136
Gwytherin 64, 148

Hackness 17
Halton Quay 87
Harlyn Bay 51, 130, 132
Hartland 28, 44, 71, 87, 118
Hay-on-Wye 69
Hebrides 13, 36, 78, 116
Helston 52, 81, 111
Henllan 134
Hentland 69
Hereford 68
Holyhead 54, 56, 57, 141
Holywell 16, 19, 64, 134, 146-8
Holywell Bay 53, 54
Huntingdon 119

Île-de-Batz 128
Inchkenneth 91
Inchmurrin 112
Inchtavannach 93
Inisglora 22
Innerwick 13, 14
Inverness 103
Iona, Isle of 10, 13, 14, 15, 20, 21, 36, 40, 46-8, 86, 91, 104, 116, plates 13, 14
Isle of Man 11, 14, 79, 109, 122, plate 19

Jarrow 10, 13, 21, plate 11
Jedburgh 21-22
Jersey 25
Jura, Isle of 103

Keighmaneigh 77
Kells 48, 86
Kent 38
Kenwyn 99
Kerry 11, 22, 23, 24, 96, 107
Kewstoke 97, 98
Keynsham 98
Kilboglashy 74
Kilbride 27
Kilbucho 17
Kilchainie 91
Kilchattan Bay 37
Kilchennich 91
Kildare 26-7, 95
Kildavanan 13
Kilkieran 43
Killaloe 53
Killin 76
Kilmacduagh 45
Kilmalkedar 10, 107, plate 10
Kilmory 103-4
Kingarth 20
Kinkardine 101
Kinsella 102

Kirkaldy 9, 140
Knapdale 103-4
Kynaston 69

Lampeter 56, 59
Lancashire 147
Landévennec 52, 81, 128
Landewednack 81
Landkey 91
Landocco 67
Land's End 138
Laneast 140-41
Lanherne 32, 72, 111
Lanivet 119
Lanmeur 117
Lantokay 90
Laois 91
Largs 94
Lastingham 38
Launceston 44, 124, 140
Lelant 72
Lemanaghan 106
Lennox 93
Lerryn 82
Lewis, Isle of 116-7
Lichfield 143
Limerick 23, 42
Lincoln 7
Lincolnshire 119
Lindisfarne 14-16, 21, 38, 48
Linkinhorne 118
Liskeard 55, 98, 119, 120
Lismore 61, 116
Little Petherick 51, 131
Lizard 52, 81, 111
Llan y Deuddeg Sant 128
Llanarmon-yn-Iâl 79
Llanasa 16, 17
Llanbadarn Fawr 125
Llanbeblig 83-4
Llanbedrog 82
Llanbeulin 128
Llancarfan 33-4
Llandaff 128, 142
Llanddaniel Fab 65
Llanddegyman 63
Llandderfel 66-7
Llanddeusant 128
Llanddewi Brefi 59
Llandeilo Fawr 63, 142
Llandough 34, 67
Llandovery 128
Llandrillo 143
Llandrillo-yn-Rhos 143
Llandudno 144

Llandysilio Island 146
Llaneilian 70
Llanelltyd 86
Llanelwy 16
Llanerchymedd 137
Llanfairpwllgwyngyll 146
Llanfyllin 116
Llangadfan 33
Llangattock-nigh-Usk 33
Llangibby-on-Usk 56
Llangiwa 98
Llangors 128-9
Llangrannog 35
Llangwyfan (Anglesey) 54
Llangwyfan (Denbighshire) 54
Llangwynnadl 82
Llangybi (Ceredigion) 56
Llangybi (Gwynedd) 56
Llangynog 111-12
Llanilltud Fawr 34, 68, 85-6, 128, 134-5
Llansadwrn 133-4
Llansanffraid 27
Llanstinan 89
Llantwit Major: see Llanilltud Fawr
Lleyn peninsula 19, 20, 33, 54, 56, 82, 99, 100, 136
Loch Cre 52
Loch Leven 139
Loch Lomond 93, 94, 112
Loch Long 93, 94
Loch Maree 103
Loch Sween 104
Loch Tay 13, 76
Lochgilphead 103
London 7, 66, 141
Looe 55, 123
Lostwithiel 82
Lough Corrib 73
Lough Derg 127
Lough Lene 74
Lough Ree 40
Louth 114
Louth, County 30,114
Lundy Island 71
Luss 93
Luxulyan 141
Lyme Regis 102

Macroom 77
Madley 68
Madron 101, 102
Malmesbury 104-5
Man, Isle of 11, 14, 79-81, 109, 122, plate 19
Marown 11, plate 19

# INDEX OF PLACE NAMES

Maughold 109-110
Mawgan Porth 110
Mawgan, Vale of 110
Mayo 22, 127
Meath 42, 61, 78, 114
Meifod 145
Melrose 21
Menai Strait 65, 145
Mendips 49
Menheniot 120
Merther Euny 72
Milton Abbey 25
Milton Eonan 13
Minehead 36
Minster 108
Moccas 69
Monasterboice 30
Monmouthshire 98
Montgomery 79
Morlaix 117
Mousehole 128
Moville 46
Much Wenlock 113
Mull, Isle of 46, 47, 91
Murrisk 127
Mylor 117

Nantes 49
Navan 73
Nectan's Kieve 118, 119
Nevern 29, 69
Newcastle-upon-Tyne 10
Newport 33, 56
Newquay 32, 49, 110, 124
North Uist 13

Oban 37
Offaly 40, 42, 115
Old Kea 91
Old Melrose 21
Onchan 14
Ossory 42, 92
Oswestry 111
Othona 38
Outer Hebrides 13
Oxford 17

Padstow 9, 51, 98, 130, 131, 132, 135, plate 5
Paisley 112, 113
Patterdale 12, plate 24
Paul 128
Peebles 100, 101
Peel 79-80, 122
Pelynt 123

Pembroke 10
Pembrokeshire 10, 29, 44, 59, 60, 63, 89, 122, 134
Penally 69, 142
Penarth 34
Penhale Sands 133
Penmaenmawr 135
Penmon 125, 136-7
Pennant Melangell 111-12, 145
Penzance 72, 101, 102, 128
Perranporth 132-3
Perranzabuloe 132
Perth 140
Perth and Kinross 28
Pettigo 127
Pittenweem 9, 75, plate 7
Plouyé 84
Pluscarden 37
Porlock 49, 69
Portmadoc 84
Portquin 71
Powys 16, 18, 79, 100, 145
Priestholm 137
Puffin Island 136
Pwhlleli 56, 82

Quimper 52

Radnor 79
Rahan 115
Ramsey Island 60, 89
Reading 7, plate 2
Redruth 72
Rhyl 16, 55
Rievaulx 121
Roche 11, plate 16
Roscrea 42, 52, 91
Roscrowther 68
Rossinver 102
Ross-on-Wye 69
Ruan Major 81
Ruthin 79

Saighir 42-3, 57, 69, 92, 132
St Albans 7, plate 1
St Asaph 16, 92
St Austell 11, 131, 141
St Bees 12, 17
St Breward 25
St Briavels 25
St Buryan 31-2, 111
St Cleer 119, 124
St Clether 44-5
St Columb Major 49
St Columb Minor 49

St David's 59-60, 63, 89, 122, 125
St Decumans 63-4
St Dominick 87
St Donats 85
St Endellion 71
St Govan's Head 10-11, plate 15
St Ives 84
St Just in Roseland 117
St Kew 67, 98, 135
St Keyne 98-9
St Levan 138
St Malo 111
St Margaret's Island 69
St Mawgan-in-Meneage 110, 111
St Mawgan-in-Pydar 32, 110, 111, 124
St Merryn 51
St Mullins 115-6
St Neot 119-20
St Neots 119
St Non's Bay 122-3
St Patrick's Isle, Peel 79-81
St-Pol-de-Léon 128
St Vigeans 73
St Winnow 82
Sancreed 32, 72, 111, 119
*Sarn Helen* 83, 125
Scarborough 38
Scattery Island 40
Scilly Isles 31, 136
Scleddau 89
Scottish Borders 100
Segontium 83
Seirkieran 42-3
Shapwick 86-7
Shrewsbury 111, 116, 146
Shropshire 112
Silchester 7, plate 2
Skail 103
Skiddaw 17, plate 23
Skye, Isle of 103, 116
Slane 126
Sligo 73, 74
Smerwick 11
Somerset 28, 35, 36, 49, 57, 63, 90, 97, plate 17
South Petherton 86
South Uist 91
Stirling 91, 94, 139
Stoke (Devon) 28, 118
Strathclyde 16, 20, 92, 93, 126
Street 90
Sutherland 103

Tara 42, 61, 126
Tarbet 94
Tenby 68, 69, 142
Tibidy, Île de 81
Tilbury 38
Tillicoultry 139
Tintagel 11, 87-8, 108, 118, plate 18
Tipperary 52
Tiree, Isle of 91
Tours 9, 42, 83, 120
Tralee 24
Tregony 55
Tresilian 141
Trossachs 94
Truro 99, 132
Tudweiliog 54
Tullamore 106, 115
Tully 27
Tywyn 32

Ullswater 12

Valle Crucis 79

Wadebridge 67, 71
Watchet 63
Waterford 61
Watergate 123
Wells 50, 63, 64
Welshpool 18, 145
Wessex 31, 50
Western Isles: *see* Hebrides
Westmeath 73
Weston-super-Mare 97
Westport 127
Wexford 102
Whitby 16, 17, 38, 39, 98
Whithorn 10, 57, 120-22, plate 12
Whithorn, Isle of 121, 122
Wicklow 95
Williton 36, 64
Wiltshire 8
Winchester 90
Wirral 147
Worlebury Hill 97
Wrexham 65
Wroxeter 18

Yatton 57
Ynys Enlli: *see* Bardsey Island
Ynys Pyr: *see* Caldey Island
Ynys Seiriol 136
York 7, 17, 121, 125
Yorkshire 17
Youghal Bay 61